The Enduring Journey
of the
USS Chesapeake

The Enduring Journey
of the
USS Chesapeake

Navigating the Common History of Three Nations

Chris Dickon

Charleston | London

THE
History
PRESS

Published by The History Press
Charleston, SC 29403
www.historypress.net

Cover image: *H.M.S.* Shannon *Leading Her Prize the American Frigate* Chesapeake *Into Halifax Harbour. Schetky, John Christian (1778–1874), Library and Archives Canada/W.H. Coverdale collection of Canadiana/C-041824.*

First published 2008

Manufactured in the United Kingdom

ISBN 978.1.59629.298.7

Library of Congress Cataloging-in-Publication Data

Dickon, Chris.
The enduring journey of the USS Chesapeake / Chris Dickon.
p. cm.
ISBN 978-1-59629-298-7
1. Chesapeake (Frigate)--History. 2. United States--History--War of 1812--Naval operations. 3. Flour mills--England--Hampshire--History. 4. Ships--Conservation and restoration--Nova Scotia--Halifax Harbour. 5. Historic preservation--Nova Scotia--Halifax Harbour. 6. Historic preservation--Case studies. I. Title.
VA65.C46D53 2008
359.8'32--dc22
                                    2008016292

CONTENTS

Preface   7
Acknowledgements   11

Chapter 1. Timbers   13
Chapter 2. A Matter of Identity   31
Chapter 3. A Funeral in Halifax   51
Chapter 4. The Plowshare   73
Chapter 5. The Return   91
Chapter 6. The Lost Cemetery   105
Chapter 7. The Souls of a Ship   123

Afterword   153

Preface

By the end of the twentieth century, the old water mill at Wickham, the County of Hampshire, England, was an exhausted hulk of a building. The River Meon, which had powered its pulleys and grindstones, still came down from the north. And Wickham itself, halfway along an old Roman road between Winchester and Chichester, continued to fulfill the terms of its 1269 charter from King Henry III as a market town. It was prosperous, to be sure. But the mill sat now unused and derelict on Bridge Street, just off the market square. And it was still the ambiguous presence in the town that it had been since 1820.

What was it exactly? Where had it come from, and where would it be going? These were more than poetic questions, for the Chesapeake Mill was built of traveling wood. Some of its beams and lintels had once grown on the coastal islands of America. They had been put together in one form and then taken apart and put together in another over the time of a circular history shared by the two Portsmouths of Virginia and England. In their construction as one of the original six frigates of the U.S. Navy, the USS *Chesapeake*, they had sailed the roiling waters of the Atlantic and the Mediterranean. They had passed through uncountable storms at sea, and sat becalmed in the sun. They had taken prizes from the enemy, and been taken prize themselves. They had seen the deaths of hundreds, and the birth of at least one child. They were most famous as a stage for one of the most storied battles in the history of sailing frigates, a brief and violent encounter off Boston Light between the *Chesapeake* and HMS *Shannon* in 1813.

Then, as a mill in Wickham, a portion of the *Chesapeake*'s timbers had given livelihood and food to the farmers, people and animals of a county in southern England for nearly two hundred years. And it was in the mill that perhaps the central moment of their lives as a collection of pieces of wood was articulated in reflections on the fates of James Lawrence, mortally wounded off Boston Light as captain of the *Chesapeake*, and of Rear Admiral Sir Philip Bowes

Vere Broke, badly wounded but not killed, as commander of the *Shannon*. Broke's biographer, a man of the cloth, had visited the hardworking mill one rainy day in the summer of 1864. He wrote,

> *On every floor, the blithe and mealy men were urging their life-sustaining toil. But, my dear reader, on one of these planks, on one of these floors, beyond all reasonable doubt, Lawrence fell, in the writhing anguish of his mortal wound…and on others Broke lay ensanguined, and his assailants dead! Thus pondering I stood, and still the busy hum went on—corn passed beneath the stones—flour poured forth, a warm, sustaining of mortal life—and merry millers passed around their kindly smile and blithesome jest.*

The biographer of 1864 had much to ponder, and the dynamics of that mental challenge would expand quietly into the twenty-first century. The naval battle of 1813 would become just a chapter in the history of these planks and beams, a history whose end cannot yet be written. For as the exhausted mill sat derelict on the River Meon near the end of the twentieth century, the sailing ship it had once been began to reemerge from history. She began her work again, and in her own way.

A sailing ship's job is to seek the winds that are most productive, and move with them through time and space. A navy frigate has the added task of pushing against complicated barriers and leaving history in her wake. For more than a millennium the job of an English water mill was to convert the perpetual motion of the rivers and tides into the "sustaining of mortal life." In this case, the timbers of the frigate *Chesapeake* and the Chesapeake Mill had, in retrospect, done splendid work.

Put together in one of the Portsmouths by a British shipbuilder in post–Revolutionary War Virginia, they formed a hybrid expression of the shipbuilder's art of two nations. An unprovoked attack upon them by the British in 1807 prompted anger in American streets, placed the first steps on the path to the War of 1812 and solidified the foundation of the U.S. Navy. It reminded Americans that theirs was a sovereign nation still needing to assert itself in the larger world.

In 1813 the timbers heard the cheers of the citizens of Boston as they sailed out to sea for battle with the *Shannon*, then heard the first uttering of the enduring U.S. Navy slogan, "Don't Give Up the Ship!" They would be honored again days later by the citizens of what was sometimes referred to as England's fourteenth colony,

Nova Scotia, as they entered Halifax Harbour in defeat. Then, departing Halifax—the geographic and emotional center of this story—they would leave behind a remembrance that would bring grown men to tears 192 years later.

Taken apart in England's Portsmouth in 1820, they would give size and shape to an English water mill, one of the most advanced industrial buildings of its time, and labor there until English bread came increasingly to be baked of wheat from the plains of Australia and North America. Then they produced cattle feed and dog food until there was no work left to be done.

Essentially abandoned at the end of the twentieth century, they took yet another turn in their journey. Though a considerable investment would be required to keep them preserved, to what end would that investment be made? After touching the histories of three nations, and in danger of being taken apart once again, or cut into shapes and purposes that would remove their historic identity, they attracted a constellation of citizens, governments, historians and commercial interests to debate and ponder upon a profound sequence of questions: What were these timbers, actually? When, if ever, did they cease to be one thing and become another thing? What is our responsibility to them? Why do we preserve history?

The deliberation went on for some years. Though many in the United States, Canada and the United Kingdom were charmed to learn the story of the mill, and as many were fervent in their advocacy of the mill's preservation as a historic place, others were ambivalent. Of the new revelations about the old mill in Wickham, England's *Daily Telegraph* editorialized in January 2004,

> *It is hard to know what to make of this information. The already considerable charm of the mill seems intensified in some way. But a plank, if dendrophiles will forgive the heresy, is a plank...If nobody told you about the floor, and you couldn't spot golden American pine by sight, you'd be none the wiser, and mystically communing with objects which have been in interesting places will only get you so far.*

Perhaps.

But how far those planks had come. And the question remained: how far were they yet to go?

ACKNOWLEDGEMENTS

This is a story of the three great nations of the Atlantic community: the United States, Canada and the United Kingdom. I've been an American all my life, a lover of Canada for half that time and now another of those fortunate travelers who has become enamored of England after just my second visit, this time in search of the story of an old navy frigate. You will meet many of the people who offered me their hospitality and assistance in the pages that follow. Guy MacLean in Halifax has been my contact with the history of a city without which the Atlantic community might be a far less happy place than it is today. And Iris Shea has helped me to better understand Melville and Deadman's Islands in Halifax with help in my research and through her book *Deadman's*, coauthored with Heather Watts. Unfailingly in Halifax, everyone I came into contact with during a glorious summer week there in 2007 was gracious and helpful. In England, I have to thank Barrie Marson of the Wickham History Society for a good lunch on Wickham Square, a spot of tea in his historic home just a few hundred feet from the Chesapeake Mill on Bridge Street and his constant research support over the year that it took to finish this book. Tony Yoward and John Silman of the Hampshire Mills Group opened their books and knowledge to me in Tony's home overlooking the tidal mill in Emsworth, and it was John who took me on the sightseer's drive from Portsmouth to Wickham, and up to the top floor of an old water mill that has received so much of his and Tony's hands-on attention. And maybe it was the great beer, but I will always remember the hospitality of Gary Carroll of the County of Hampshire's Department of Estates Planning, who picked me up on his way home from a meeting in Winchester, took me for a pint in a great pub and drove me back to my hotel in Portsmouth during afternoon rush hour. Also in England, Adriane de Savorgnani at the U.S. Embassy in London has been as persistent a help as she has been an advocate for the USS *Chesapeake*. And Eric Walker has become a telephone and postal mail friend, as he is a good English friend to the old American frigate.

ACKNOWLEDGEMENTS

This book has been written on the western branch of the Elizabeth River in Portsmouth, Virginia, just a few miles by rowboat from the place of the Chesapeake's launching in 1799. Here in Hampton Roads, I am fortunate to live among some of the best of the country's naval history organizations. My thanks to the Hampton Roads Naval Museum in Norfolk, to Corey Thornton of the Naval Shipyard Museum in Portsmouth and to Bill Cogar of the Mariners' Museum in Newport News. The Mariners', in particular, is a remarkable world resource for naval history. The depths of its print, art and photo archives seem like a bottomless sea. My special thanks go to Claudia Jew, director of photographic services at the Mariners' Museum, whose support from the beginning has carried me through to the end. And to Jeff Macechak of the Burlington County (New Jersey) Historical Society, the best representative that the fallen naval hero James Lawrence could hope to have in modern times.

All of those above have graciously read drafts of the parts of the book in which they are quoted. Their comments and fact-checking have been valuable and appreciated. And it was Barrie Marson who pointed out that if this was to be a book to be shared by three countries, it should not be limited to just one in its use of terms and spellings. Thus, when we are in America, for example, we'll pay attention to its *harbors*, but while in Canada or England we'll travel in their *harbours*. Finally, this book bows down to another book. It was a reading of Ian Toll's *Six Frigates* that brought all of early American history to life for me as I started to consider this book—a true inspiration and a great read.

Chapter i

Timbers

When, in the year 2004, a British newspaper posed the appropriately provocative question as to the true worth of a collection of pieces of wood that had once been a portion of a U.S. Navy frigate, it unwittingly compounded a poetic observation first made more than three hundred years earlier. With all due respect to dendrophiles, wrote the *Daily Telegraph* of January 24, a piece of wood may ultimately be nothing more than a piece of wood.

In the context of the modern environmental movement, "dendrophile" is a different version of the term "tree hugger," and in some mocking uses of the word it takes on a connotation of an interaction with trees that goes beyond mere hugging.

In the late 1600s, the now famed British diarist Samuel Pepys was better known as an effective naval administrator at a time when the British navy began to deal with a problem it would never quite solve: the difficulty of obtaining the proper wood for the masts, spars and timbers of its far-reaching flotilla of fighting ships. He advised that his friend Robert Plott study the problem from his perspective as an Oxford-trained natural historian.

"All trees in the spring season and some time after," wrote Plott in an *Advice* to the king, "are pregnant, and spend themselves in the production of leaves and fruits, and so become weaker than at other times of the year." He observed that trees felled in those months would be turgid with the fluids of life, but that those fluids would eventually putrify, "leaving the tree full of cavities, which render the timber weak." A ship timber, especially a mast timber, had to be captured at just the right moment in the life of a tree to be of the proper size, sufficiently pliable and strong. But the relatively temperate climate of Great Britain was not always conducive to allowing the time and temperatures needed for the proper seasoning of the wood.

This was a problem, because ship timbers were the oil of their day. Without them the world would not have been easily explored and settled. Roaming that world, as it did, however, the Royal

Navy could find the best building materials for its ships in other lands and climates. The colonies of North America were an abundant source beginning in 1609. Timbers were exported from the Jamestown Colony in Virginia for a few years, until the settlers gained a preference for growing tobacco. Then it was the pine forests north of New Hampshire and into Maine that provided wood, most of it distributed to British holdings in the Atlantic and Caribbean from Portsmouth, New Hampshire, and Falmouth (now Portland), Maine. But the first conflicts of the Revolutionary War in 1775 changed everything. The colonists cut off British supplies of American timber, and Falmouth was, in turn, burned to the ground by the English enemy. After the war, North American wood had to come increasingly from New Brunswick and Quebec, exported through Halifax. The need was dire. The most famous of the British ships of the line, the 104-gun HMS *Victory*, launched in 1765, was constructed of an estimated six thousand trees yielded from one hundred acres of forest. In 1801, the Royal Navy estimated the requirement of eighteen thousand tons of timber and five hundred masts for maintenance and construction of the fleet. And the British, once assured of endless supplies of naval wood in one way or another, necessarily began to get smarter about how they treated, preserved, used and even recycled the wood that was still available to them.

In 1724, some years after the publication of his novel *Robinson Crusoe*, the British author Daniel Defoe set out to describe in great detail the features of the County of Hampshire, the historic seat of British naval power, anchored by the harbour at Portsmouth, Britain's gateway to the oceans of the world.

Defoe wrote,

> *The situation of this place is such that it is chosen, as may well be said, for the best security to the navy above all the places in Britain; the entrance into the harbour is safe, but very narrow, guarded on both sides by terrible platforms of cannon…'tis evident, in the opinion of all that I have met with, that the greatest fleet of ships that ever were in the hands of one nation at a time, would not pretend, if they had not an army also on shoar, to attack the whole work, to force their entrance into the harbour at Portsmouth.*

The harbour, formed of the ancient Solent River Valley that had widened and deepened over thousands of years, had served

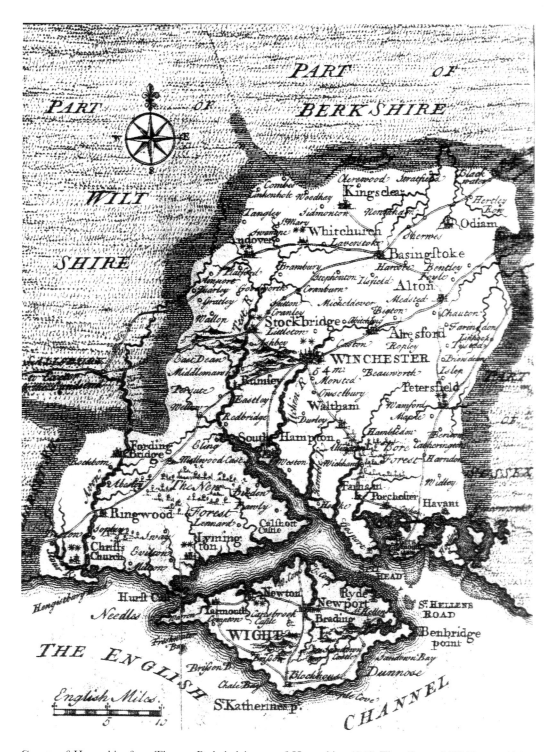

County of Hampshire from Thomas Badeslade's map of Hampshire, 1742. The village of Wickham, which would become the final resting place of the remains of the USS *Chesapeake*, sits north of Farnham. *Courtesy Old Hampshire Map Site, Internet.*

as a key base of the Roman Empire and the site of its largest fortress in northwest Europe. Portchester Castle was built strongly enough that its walls still stand into the twenty-first century. From the seventeenth century the harbour developed in its service to the British Empire as the home of advanced naval dockyards, stores and hospitals, forming what may have been the largest British industrial enterprise before the Industrial Revolution. The sailing ships they produced and provisioned would eventually come to be called "The Wooden Walls" of England.

"These docks and yards," Defoe observed, "are now like a town by themselves, and are a kind of marine corporation, or a government of their own kind within themselves." Defoe continued his exploration of the Solent on the ferries that traveled to Southampton, past the Hamble and Meon Rivers and over to Gosport, which stood face to face with Portsmouth across the water.

When a group of 104 Englishmen and boys entered North America's Chesapeake Bay in 1607 and sailed up the James River to form the Jamestown settlement, they were met with every conceivable barrier to the success of their venture. Whatever they may have expected, this was not England reborn. The water was mostly unsuitable for drinking, and the mosquitoes were impossible to bear. Good agricultural land was sparse, and hunting in the tidal lands and marshes was difficult. The native Indians were hostile.

It was no wonder that as the region of the lower Chesapeake Bay developed in the following years, it became modeled in many respects on the England left behind. Naval historian James Thomas of the University of Portsmouth in England points to Portsmouth,

The Portsmouth Dockyards, 1754. The ship on the far right is HMS *Neptune*. *Portsmouth and Sunderland Newspapers, the* News, *Portsmouth. www. portsmouth.co.uk.*

New Hampshire, and Portsmouth, Virginia (though not officially named until 1752), as examples. "Somehow, part of you is still where you left from," he said. "What these people must have done was to actually take themselves and their families to the new communities and set about recreating what they knew back home."

Thus, the communities that developed in the lower bay region took on the names of familiar places. Norfolk County, England, named for the "north folk" of East Anglia, gave its name to Norfolk County (now city), Virginia. The Isle of Wight, touched by the Solent in England, gave its name to a county on the lower James River. Surrey County, England, became Surry County, Virginia. Northamptonshire (the "shire of the homestead") in the English Midlands gave its name to Northampton County on the lower eastern shore of Virginia. Newport News, Virginia, assumed its name, by one accounting of history, as the place to which Christopher Newport, captain of the Jamestown-bound *Susan Constant*, delivered the news from home after each of his journeys back and forth across the Atlantic. The harbor, and the entire region, gained a two-word name: *Hampton*, after the Third Earl of Southampton, and *Roads*, from the nautical meaning of road as "a place less sheltered than a harbor where ships may ride at anchor." Hampton Roads would remain a name for the region, known more

Portsmouth Harbour and the Solent, circa 1895. The HMS *Victory* (center) launched in 1765, would remain in the harbour into the twenty-first century, a reminder of England's historic naval superiority. *Library of Congress, Prints & Photographs Division, Photochrom Collection.*

to the locals than to the world at large, except for the shipping community, into the twenty-first century.

When, eventually, the new colony began to get firmly into the necessary business of shipbuilding and repair, the shipyard that developed took on the name of Gosport in the Solent. "Gosport" was either a medieval word for "port of geese" or else it came from a phrase uttered by a twelfth-century sea captain who found refuge from a bad storm in the safety of the Solent. "God's port our haven," he was reported to have exclaimed.

A difference between the two Gosports might have portended the dance of opposites, the conflicts and alliances, yet to unfold in the history of England and America. The town of Gosport in England sat across the harbour from Portsmouth and its large naval yards. In Virginia, the Gosport naval yard sat on the Elizabeth River, named for Princess Elizabeth Stuart (1596–1660), the daughter of King James I of England. It would eventually become part of Portsmouth, and sit across the harbor from Norfolk.

The Gosport, Virginia Shipyard was established under British flag by Andrew Sprowle in 1767. Arriving in Virginia about 1735, he brought with him the experience of working in the great shipyards of Glasgow and London, and he knew that those yards

Hampton Roads from a map dedicated to Right Honourable George Dunk, Earl of Halifax, and other commissioners for trade and plantations, dated 1775. Jamestown sits on the north shore of the curve in the James River. The Gosport Shipyard sat at the confluence of the southern and eastern branches of the Elizabeth River. *Kirn Library, Norfolk, Sargeant Memorial Room.*

needed to be duplicated in the colonies if England were to continue its domination of the seas. The yard was built on origins going back to the early 1600s. To make his yard more attractive to British sea captains, he gave it the name Gosport, reminiscent of the Solent and home. His shipyard became the largest, perhaps the most modern, in the colonies. And the most notable of its shipwrights in the early years would be the Englishman Josiah Fox.

By the time Fox arrived in America in 1793, the young history of the Gosport Shipyard had been one of great success and wrenching change. Sprowle had grown very wealthy as a repairer and supplier of the naval and commercial ships of Great Britain. His shipyard had given shelter to the British royal governor of Virginia and fellow Scotsman, Lord Dunmore, as Dunmore's continuous clashes with the Virginia Assembly before the Revolutionary War pushed him into the first steps of fleeing from the country in July 1776. When Dunmore departed, the Tory Andrew Sprowle went with him, though he got only as far as Gwynn's Island near Gloucester County, where he died under mysterious circumstances.

Gosport was taken over by the Virginia state navy, supporting American naval needs of the Revolutionary War up until 1779, when the British tried to retake the vital shipyard, but only succeeded in burning it to the ground. Through auctions of former Tory properties, Virginia took official possession of the yard in 1780, but with the end of the war in 1783 the Virginia navy was disbanded and Gosport fell into disuse until the arrival in 1794 of Josiah Fox, and the beginning of the centuries-long journey of the USS *Chesapeake*.

In that year the world of the oceans between America and Europe, and the ships that sailed upon them, had been in chaos

In one of the earliest pictures of the Gosport yard, circa 1795, the HMS *Thetis* is serviced by careening, or turning a ship on its side for cleaning, caulking or repairing. *Kirn Library, Norfolk, Sargeant Memorial Room.*

for some time, a place where every collection of unidentified masts on the far horizon could be the portent of doom and disaster. American ships had much to trade with the larger world, but prewar protection offered them by the British navy had changed to hostility. As American merchant ships ventured into the Mediterranean, they were met with perhaps the most fearsome enemy a sailing ship could come up against: the pirates of the Barbary States of Morocco, Tunis, Tripoli and Algiers. With little in the way of natural economic resources, the Islamic nations enriched themselves from the ships of Europe, England and America that passed through the Straits of Gibraltar, and the usual protocols of naval interaction among combatants didn't apply. No matter whether you were a common sailor or an officer, if you were captured in one of these encounters you could expect, with some exceptions, an immediate, and probably eternal, future as a slave in chains, a life of eternal hard labor, hunger, imprisonment and beatings. Your only hope, if you had one at all, was that you be ransomed or rescued, either action at tremendous cost.

The pirates were an almost insurmountable impediment to a new nation beginning to assert itself in the larger world, *almost* because there was one way to keep them at bay and in port—the payment of tribute in cash and goods to Barbary States. It was, in fact, an economic system that had existed among the nations of the Mediterranean for centuries. The decision had to be made as to whether it was easier and cheaper to pay the pirates or fight them, and the former usually won the day. And in the case of Great Britain, still ruler of the seas and easily capable of pounding the pirates back to the harbors of their offending nations, it might be said that it was an economic system that did more harm to rival nations than to themselves.

Pay or fight was the argument in America. The problem was complicated by the French Revolution that had begun in 1789 and the reaction against it by surrounding nations, leading to the European War of 1792 and then to the Napoleonic Wars, which would go on until 1815. The potential market for American goods and resources in the warring nations was limitless. It was difficult enough to trade those exports in the midst of fighting navies, but the pirates were the final slam of the doorway to international economic expansion.

The decision was made to fight, and, after a long national debate about what the government could and should afford, and what a concentrated naval force could accomplish, President Washington signed an act of Congress authorizing the purchase or construction of six frigates at a budgeted cost of $688,888. The date was March 27, 1794, the conception, if not the birthday, of the U.S. Navy. The decision was made to build the frigates, and Washington directed that the construction take place in six shipyards, north to south: Portsmouth, New Hampshire; Boston; New York; Philadelphia; Baltimore; and Norfolk (Gosport). The six were first named A, B, C, D, E and F. The president then gave proper names to five of the ships: *Congress*, *Constellation*, *Constitution*, *President* and *United States*. D would maintain its official, lackluster name for some time. And even as the *Chesapeake*, as she would eventually be named, she would often be thought of as the orphan, the runt of the litter, the unlucky ship.

The frigates were designed and built under the supervision of Joshua Humphreys of Philadelphia. Though a Quaker, he had no compunction about building warships. He determined that his ships would be superior in every way to the best of the European frigates: larger, faster, more nimble, more fire power and made of the best materials by the most skilled of workers.

But then there was the matter of timbers. And after that there was the matter of Josiah Fox.

If there was ever a place where ship timbers could be harvested that were already seasoned by the forces of the environment in which they would be asked to do their work, it was St. Simons Island, off the coast of Georgia. Emerging from the thawing of the last ice age, it became a place of artesian wells and thick foliage. Its marshes were fed twice daily by the sea, and, providentially perhaps, it was situated in a way that gave its trees protection from hurricanes, while they thrived on coastal winds and fogs. It had been the home of agricultural Indians and Spanish missionaries, then English colonists (many of them from the debtors' prisons of London) and then the Spanish once again.

Joshua Humphreys remarked that the quality of the timbers in the Philadelphia shipyard "is greatly superior to any in Europe, and the best that have ever come to this place." Secretary of the Navy Benjamin Stoddart said that the live oaks of St. Simons would be indispensable in those portions of the frigates most susceptible to decay, and predicted that they would have lifetimes exceeding fifty years.

The problem was that St. Simons refused to give them up without a fight. Humphreys had estimated that it would take fifty-five men forty-eight days to cut the oak, cedar and pine needed for a single frigate. The live oaks, in particular, at St. Simons would be large enough to be cut into framing for the large ships, and each of the frigates would consume several hundred of them. Boston shipwright John Morgan was sent to harvest and cut the trees, but when he arrived in the late summer of 1794 he found them in a hellish swampland with a mud floor, soaked in rain and thick with mosquitoes.

The labor force that would be put to the task was a good one, but the carpenters and axe-men came from cool New England, and soon after their arrival many of them lay prostrate in heat and illness. Most of those who recovered returned to New England by Christmas, never to return. On October 21, 1794, Morgan wrote to Humphreys: "If I am to stay here until all the timber has been cut I shall be dead…I cannot stand it…if you was here you would curse live oak."

When the commander of the yet-to-be-built USS *United States* traveled from Philadelphia to assess the situation in Georgia, he found virtually no labor force and no wood yet cut. A slave workforce was brought in to clear roads and make the environment

Contemporary oaks on St. Simons Island, believed to date to the early nineteenth century. The Coastal Georgia Experience.

more workable. But the tallest oaks required were still the most inaccessible, and those that could not be floated off the island had to be dragged by oxen over an unforgiving land of roots and vines. Before the year was out, most of the oxen had died in the effort. The building plan was delayed.

Then, a further delay was prompted by a turn of events in the Mediterranean. A condition of the funding for the six frigates was that if peace should be attained with the Barbary States, their construction would stop. And, almost by surprise, a negotiated peace involving the payment of nearly $1 million to Algiers was announced in October 1795. It did not seem to be applicable to all of the Barbary States, however, especially Morocco, and the decision was made to proceed with the construction of just three of the frigates: *Constitution*, *United States* and *Constellation*. Work already done on the other three was to be stopped in place.

The *United States* was grounded and severely damaged by her launching in May 1797. Repairs were delayed by the outbreak of yellow fever in Philadelphia, and as soon as it was possible, the ship was moved away from the shipyard and downriver to get her away from the city. The *Constellation* was launched successfully in Baltimore in September of that year, but the finishing and rigging that was to take place in the Patapsco River was also halted by the yellow fever in Fells Point, and the ship spent the winter in the harbor while its builders feared that she might be pushed aground by the harsh weather of the season. In the first attempt to launch the *Constitution* in Boston, with President James Madison in attendance, she barely got down the ways before grinding to a halt. It took two more attempts over several weeks to get her in the water. Eventually, all three ships were underway, referred to in the *Norfolk (Virginia) Weekly Journal* of September 19, 1798, as the "Floating Castles" of the United States.

Design and construction of what would be named *Chesapeake* had begun with the Naval Act of 1794, and stopped on March 15, 1796. Peace with Barbary pirates, however, had not diminished the problems of American merchant ships as they traveled the world. The British were still prickly about American trade, and it was now French privateers who took American ships and sailors with impunity, even snatching them from American rivers and harbors. In December 1796, President George Washington, in his final address to Congress, warned of a future war with Europe that might find American shipping interests still unprotected, and recommended that the nation "set about the gradual creation of a navy." Washington's successor, John Adams, agreed, and on April

A montage summarizing the life of Josiah Fox, pictured as a boy in 1771 and as an old man. Handwriting summarizes his many accomplishments. It refers to the *Chesapeake* as a forty-four-gun frigate, though that original plan for the ship was later reduced to thirty-eight. *The Mariners' Museum, Newport News, Virginia.*

30, 1798, a U.S. Navy, independent from the army, was created. Completion was authorized for all six of the original frigates, and money was appropriated for the building of another twenty-four warships ranging in size from eighteen to thirty-two guns.

It was England's continuing quest for usable timbers that brought Josiah Fox to America in late 1793. Born in Falmouth, Cornwall, in 1763, he was apprenticed at age eighteen in the Royal Navy Dockyards at Plymouth. Then, as a shipwright, he traveled across the Atlantic to investigate the supply and availability of American timbers, with a particular interest in live oak and red cedar. His talents soon led to his inclusion in the group of architects and builders assigned to the creation of the six frigates, the only one of the group trained in Great Britain. He would serve as a naval architect under four presidents.

NOTES:

Like Joshua Humphreys, Fox was a Quaker, though he had been disowned by the Philadelphia meeting because of his involvement in ships of war. And he was very much his own man, somewhat eccentric and a keeper of notes. As chief naval architect at the Gosport Shipyard, he had laid the keel of the *Chesapeake* before the suspension of construction in 1796, and set about completing her construction in December of 1798. His charge was to have the ship in the water within twelve months, while running a shipyard that was already occupied with the needs of existing ships. Therein lay the beginning of the *Chesapeake*'s reputation as an outrider, sometimes called "an odd duck," among the six frigates.

All six had been designed by Joshua Humphreys, but the plan that would have him overseeing the fulfillment of his design by strong-willed shipbuilders in five other locations had not been well conceived. And the three Humphreys-designed ships already

184-31

A letter dated April 24, 1797, from Johsua Humphreys to George Washington following up on a discussion about a water pump, and promising the launch of the USS *United States* within one month. *Library of Congress.*

Differing accounts offer differing dimensions for the USS *Chesapeake* at launch. The most prevalent state that she was 152 feet, 6 inches long; with a beam of 40 feet, 11 inches; a gun deck of 158 feet, 8 inches; 38 guns; weighed 1,244 tons; and cost $220,678. Accounts of subsequent events in her history would often vary in describing the number of guns she carried.

launched were not without mixed reviews. The *United States* was judged fast and nimble, but perhaps top-heavy. The *Constellation* was criticized as weakened by a disproportion between its width and length. The *Constitution* was deemed to draw too much water for U.S. harbors. Of course, all such judgments were influenced by the egos and rivalries of those making them, and by 1798, a rivalry between the two Quakers, Humphreys and Fox, had turned into a war of words recorded in history in the equivalent of an ongoing and angry exchange of memos. In one exchange, Fox referred to himself as a "Naval Constructor," and Humphreys replied, "I cannot receive hereafter or attend to any directions from you, although directed by the Secretary of War, while you style yourself 'Naval Constructor.' You must know that my station in the service of the United States requires no direction from a 'Naval Constructor.'"

Though Fox had been originally hired as draftsman for Humphreys's designs, he did not believe in those designs, and was evidently not shy in saying so. When the task fell upon him to finish the construction of the *Chesapeake* in less than one year, he was given the opportunity—by pleading the press of time, a shortage of labor and continuing timber problems—to redesign the ship according to his own calculations. Her stern would be redesigned and she would be reduced in size. In the final plan she would be 152 feet and 6 inches in length at the waterline (*Constitution* was 175 feet), almost 41

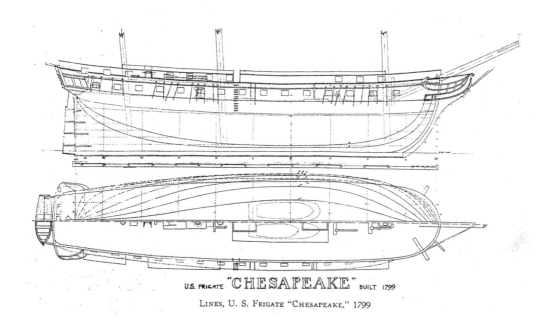

LINES, U. S. FRIGATE "CHESAPEAKE," 1799

feet at the beam and would weigh 1,244 tons. Most important for a fighting ship, the 44 guns of the original plan were reduced to 38.

The ship was ready for launch a few days short of a year's building. Her keel timbers may have originated in part at St. Simons Island, but the rest of her wood had to come from wherever it could be found. Often, timbers intended for the *Chesapeake* would be redirected from Gosport to Baltimore for continuing work on the *Constellation*. But it was in the matter of labor that the construction of the *Chesapeake*, true to the spirit of the outrider, helped to open up a new kind of idea. It wasn't only that the Quaker Josiah Fox was a builder of warships; he was also an owner of slaves in late eighteenth-century Virginia, and the *Chesapeake* was built with a lot of slave labor. Fox bought the slaves, set them to work at a fixed rate of compensation and when they had worked out their purchase price he set them free.

Over the years since then, the launching of the USS *Chesapeake* has been seen by some historians as an ominous harbinger of her future, though it seems to be a view with a bias that isn't easily understood. Perhaps it came from a perception that the ship had been orphaned from the family of "the six frigates" by the animosity between Joshua Humphreys and Josiah Fox. On her launch day of December 1, 1799, she would move only a few

An eighteen-pounder cannon dated 1801, Seville, Spain, sets its aim from the modern Portsmouth waterfront at the private Norfolk Ship Repair yard known as Norshipco. *City of Portsmouth, Virginia.*

Fates and Fortunes

USS CHESAPEAKE
–Captured by
the British, 1813.
Broken up and a
portion converted to
a water mill, 1820.

USS CONGRESS
–Unfit for naval
service and broken
up by U.S. Navy,
1834.

USS CONSTITUTION
–After many
restorations, still in
Boston Harbor.

USS CONSTELLATION
–Broken up by
U.S. Navy, 1853. A
second *Constellation*
was built in 1854,
perhaps using eight
pieces of the original
frigate. The true
provenance of the
Constellation currently
in Baltimore Harbor
is historically
controversial.

USS PRESIDENT
–Captured by
the British, 1815.
Broken up at
Portsmouth,
England, in 1818.

USS UNITED STATES
–Seized in Norfolk
by the Confederate
States Navy, 1861.
Recovered by Union
forces in 1862 and
broken up in 1865.

feet down the ways, impeded by cold weather and frozen tallow. A footnote in history suggests, but does not document, that a worker in the yard was killed in the process. On the following day, reported the *Norfolk Herald* of December 3, "at half past one o'clock, in the presence of a great concourse of people, was safely launched into her element the United States frigate *Chesapeake*."

Fully fitted, she finally got underway on May 22, 1800. "As she passed the shipping that lay in the harbor," the newspaper reported, "she fired a salute of 13 guns, which was handsomely returned by every vessel that mounted a gun…the wharves and houses next to the river were lined with people, who with three cheers welcomed her as she passed the town point."

In 1814, Josiah Fox, restored to the good graces of the Quakers, settled in an Ohio home thought to have been a replica of his ancestral home in Cornwall. He is buried near the Old Concord Meeting House in Colerain, near Cincinnati.

Despite the cheers in her honor as she sailed up the river toward whatever the future might hold, the *Chesapeake* would never seem to gain the good graces of history and historians. Not even two hundred years would soften an initial, and seemingly unfair, judgment of her perceived shortcomings. "In some ships every accident is considered the work of a malevolent star," wrote the naval historian Captain Edward Beach in 2002, "some evil spirit of bad luck hovering over her. Such was the case with the *Chesapeake*… and it may have begun, because, of the original six ships, she was the runt of the litter."

The judgment then and now is inexplicable. Other of the ships had problems at launch. All of them were criticized for some fault or another, and all would meet varying degrees of success in battle. Two would be captured by the British. One of them, the USS *President*, would eventually be broken apart in England, her timbers scattered to the winds that had once filled her sails. The *Chesapeake*, too, would be broken in England, but in a way that would set her on a different course than the others. Indeed, whatever the nature of the star that hovered above her, it would stay in place into the twenty-first century—with a signed leasehold on the twenty-second.

The USS *Chesapeake. Wilson History Room, Portsmouth (Virginia) Public Library.*

CHAPTER 2

A MATTER OF IDENTITY

In 1807, America was awakened from something of a post-Revolutionary slumber. Having asserted itself in the successful war against its parent nation, it had then seemed to allow the energy of that revolution to dwindle, and the remnants of British rule and influence to linger.

In that year, the Gosport Shipyard at Portsmouth was commanded by Stephen Decatur Jr. Eight years later he would surrender the USS *President* to the British off Long Island, New York, and five years beyond that he would be killed in a duel with an embittered former captain of the USS *Chesapeake*, James Barron. In 1804, however, Stephen Decatur became one of the nation's first, and wildly celebrated, naval heroes when, once again, America would be challenged by the pirate states just on the other side of the Straits of Gibraltar.

At about the time that the *Chesapeake* had been first sent out to sea, the U.S. Navy was on its way to shutting down its operations for lack of something to do. Problems with France had pretty much ended with the conclusion of what was known as the Quasi-War, a sort of undeclared conflict over treaties between the two nations that was played out mainly at sea. The *Chesapeake* ended up patrolling threats to American shipping in the Caribbean, and, like a modern-day cruise ship, made regular rounds at St. Kitts, St. Thomas and St. Bart's. There were occasional distractions. One day in November of 1800 the *Chesapeake* and the *President* found themselves alone on a sea bereft of enemies, and engaged in a simple race of speed. The *Chesapeake* lost the race, but soon after captured an enemy privateer at the end of a fifty-hour chase.

By 1801 the navy had grown in its number of ships and sailors, and it was consuming almost half of the federal budget. When the new president, Thomas Jefferson, took office in that year he was not in disagreement with a congressional order of March 3 establishing a peacetime navy. In essence, it directed that most of the navy, with the exception of the six frigates, be put in ordinary,

Searching for Bermuda

It was a very difficult place to find, lying so low in the water, but very often when a light breeze is blowing off the land in the evening, one can scent the cedars growing there before he sees them.

–Charles Loftus, *My Youth by Sea and Land, 1809–1816*

or sold outright, and that personnel be fired or put on half pay in certain circumstances.

It was a plan that most everyone could agree upon, but ten days later it was turned on its ear by a letter from the Barbary Coast to Secretary of State James Madison. Previous agreements notwithstanding, stated the ruler of Tripoli, a substantial increase in the payment of tribute was required, or war would be declared upon the United States in six months' time. The letter, however, had arrived five months after its signing, and when Jefferson dispatched a small fleet of ships to observe the situation they found upon arrival that war had indeed been proclaimed several weeks earlier. Without further instruction, the fleet set up a blockade of the Tripolitan harbor. Tensions were not resolved by the end of the year, and in the American debate as to whether to pay increased tribute or to fight back, at a greater expense, the latter view prevailed. A new squadron of ships was sent east to blockade Tripoli and assist American ships, with the *Chesapeake* as flagship under Commodore Richard Morris.

The journey did not go well. Rough weather did severe damage to her masts and spars, and at Gibraltar her mainmast was found to be of rotten wood. "I never was at sea in so uneasy a ship," Commodore Morris declared. But if the *Chesapeake* had been bandied about by the sea, Morris himself proved to be under the influence of another of nature's forces in the form of his wife Anne, who was onboard with their young son Gerard. The carrying of women aboard navy ships was forbidden, though exceptions were made in the cases of family members of commanding officers. And at this point in her career the *Chesapeake* would enter the lore of naval history in regard to its women, both known and mysterious.

The ship seemed to languish under repair at Gibraltar, a time viewed by junior officers as perhaps more under the command of the "commodoress" than the commodore. Then the ship was sailed to Malta for further repairs, where Mrs. Morris gave birth to a son in the hospital at Valetta. But the credible account of a midshipman, Henry Wadsworth, held that another child had been born in the boatswain's storeroom while the ship was at sea. The infant, Melancthon Woolsey Low, was the son of Captain of the Forecastle James Low. Wadsworth's account of his baptism mentions four other women on the ship as wives of officers.

Many years later, an official investigation by the navy of the history of women on its early ships found no record of the existence of any of them on the *Chesapeake* (or the male child Melancthon). It

In Ordinary

Vessels in ordinary are those out of actual use, commonly dismasted, and occasionally roofed over, to protect them from the weather. They are congregated near the several dockyards, where their masts and gear be ready for their immediate fitting for sea when required.

–Chambers's Encyclopedia: A Dictionary of Universal Knowledge for the People, 1870

speculated that they may have been wives gained in the course of the frigate's travels, but kept off the books.

The *Chesapeake* played no remarkable role in the Tripolitan blockade. Morris and others were held hostage by the Algerian leader in Tunis for a few days in relation to another matter, but were released without incident. Eventually, the *Chesapeake* was ordered to return home. Among her passengers was Stephen Decatur, sent home as a precaution against the threat of murder charges by Maltese authorities after his participation as a second in a fatal duel. The new captain of the *Chesapeake* for her return trip was James Barron.

Stephen Decatur was soon to return to the Mediterranean, and to engage in what even the British Admiral Lord Nelson was to call "the most bold and daring act of the age." In late October 1803, the USS *Philadelphia* had become grounded on a reef in Tripoli Harbor as the result of a skirmish with a Tripolitan ship. No effort or height of tide succeeded in freeing her, and, hopelessly stuck in place, her officers and crew were eventually taken to imprisonment in the city. Soon refloated by her captors, the restoration process was begun that would turn her into *The Gift of Allah*. She would have become one of the most effective of Tripolitan fighting frigates, and in December a decision was made by American Commodore Edward Preble that if she could not be retaken, she would have to be destroyed.

Many volunteered to lead the dangerous mission, but Stephen Decatur was chosen. Sailing in a captured coastal trading ship, Decatur and eighty men and officers sailed up to the *Philadelphia* and pleaded for help. An Arabic-speaking harbor pilot among them told of damage done to the little trader in bad storms, and asked if the smaller ship could tie up to the frigate for the night.

The ruse succeeded. Decatur managed to regain the *Philadelphia*, and his men moved to all portions of the ship, setting it afire almost methodically, and then all escaped without serious injury back into the old trader. In his *History of the Navy of the United States*, the author and naval historian James Fenimore Cooper reported the result:

> *The spectacle that followed is described as having been both beautiful and sublime. The entire bay was illuminated by the conflagration, the roar of cannon was constant, and Tripoli was in a clamour. The appearance of the ship was, in the highest degree, magnificent; and, to add to the effect, as her guns heated, they began to go off. Owing to the shift of wind, and the position*

Commodore Daniel Todd Patterson was in command of the Mediterranean Squadron, 1832–33, U.S.S. *United States*, flagship. He took his wife and his daughter George Ann with him and apparently they remained on shipboard throughout the cruise. They are mentioned several times by Midshipman Stuyvesant Fish who kept a journal of the cruise of the *United States*. Young Fish took a dim view of ladies on board naval ships, speaking of Mrs. Patterson and her daughter thus: "The females have been already wished home a thousand times by every officer, as they have already given difficulty and will cause, eventually, the cruise to be disagreeable. They rule when the ship is to sail, already." –"Women in the Navy," Operational Archives Branch, Naval Historical Center, Washington, D.C.

into which she had tended, she, in some measure, returned the enemy's fire, as one of her broadsides was discharged in the direction of the town, and the other towards Fort English. The most singular effect of this conflagration was on board the ship, where the flames, having run up the rigging and masts, collected under the tops, and fell over, giving the whole the appearance of glowing columns and fiery capitals.

The winds then took Decatur out of the harbor, where he boarded a larger brigantine and set sail for Syracuse, on the far side of Sicily, arriving three days later.

The Tripolitan War came to a conclusion in 1805. Hastened in part by the work of the United States Marines, it inspired the lines of the Marine Hymn: "From the halls of Montezuma to the shores of Tripoli/We will fight our country's battles on the land as on the sea."

The Star-Spangled Flag
Around 1804–05 the poet Francis Scott Key wrote a poem in honor of Stephen Decatur's actions in the Tripolitan War. It included the words "Star Spangled Flag" and was soon made into a song, set to the tune of "Anacreon in Heaven," a popular song in the gentlemen's clubs of Great Britain. While watching the Battle of Fort McHenry on September 14, 1814, Key rewrote the song, changed "flag" to "banner" and created the U.S. national anthem.

The war against the pirates had taken place against the more complicated backdrop of the continuing Napoleonic Wars that would involve most of Europe and Russia. On the seas, the battles were mostly between Britain and France, and those who fought those battles lived in a world of confusing identities and allegiances. Even Americans, though they did not have a stake in the fight, were drawn into the maelstrom through the brutal mechanism of impressment.

If a navy needed a continuing supply of timbers to stay afloat, it also needed an unending supply of men to move it forward into battle. If those sailors could not be recruited, they would instead be captured and impressed into servitude. Impressment was a practice dating back to medieval times. Britain was not its sole practitioner, but the size and range of the Royal Navy made it the most notorious, and it seemed to be relentless in doing what it had to do to man its ships. Statistically, the need for impressment was obvious. The British had estimated that in 1775 the colonies held a seagoing labor force of ten thousand men, ostensibly no longer available to their ships after the Revolution. Not only were practicing sailors impressed from the military and commercial ships of other nations captured at sea, but press gangs also roamed docks and public houses, and even plucked men out of the wailing arms of their families for forced service in His Majesty's Navy. If a given ship arrived in port without enough crew, it might assemble a gang of its toughest sailors to go into town and bring back the required number of hands.

Decatur's Conflict with the Algerine at Tripoli. The engraving, after a painting by Alonzo Chappel, is often identified as associated with the boarding of USS *Philadelphia.* It may actually depict the fight to capture a Tripolitan gunboat on August 3, 1804. *The Mariners' Museum, Newport News, Virginia.*

Burning of the Frigate Philadelphia *in the Harbour of Tripoli, 16th Feb. 1804, by 70 Gallant Tars of* Columbia *commanded by Lieut. Decatur.* The ketch *Intrepid*, at left, leaves Tripoli Harbor after her crew had boarded the *Philadelphia* and set the ship ablaze. *The Mariners' Museum, Newport News, Virginia.*

The Battle of Trafalgar, fought on October 21, 1805, was one of the most important sea battles of the Napoleonic Wars, and is a marker of British history. Admiral Lord Horatio Nelson of the HMS *Victory* led twenty-seven ships of the Royal Navy against a French and Spanish fleet of thirty-three ships off the coast of Spain. Twenty-two enemy ships were lost, while all British ships survived, though some were severely damaged. Lord Nelson was mortally wounded, and instantly became a hero in the history of England. British fighting ships were called "The Wooden Walls of England," and the HMS *Victory* would become a timeless symbol, along with Lord Nelson, of the historic force of the Royal Navy.

It was not uncommon for many of those so captured to jump ship when the opportunity arose and, finding themselves far from home, to sign on with a competing naval force that might help them to return to their origins. As regards the United States and Britain, the confusion of identity was enlarged by the ability of sailors to blend into the common language of two nations. Many members of the low-paying and notoriously brutal British navy opted to join

the U.S. Navy when they could, as conditions were better and pay was higher. Compounding the problem was the easy availability to British seamen of fake documents of American citizenship, further compounded by the result that British naval authorities saw few of the documents, real or fake, as reliable. Beyond that, they refused to accept that naturalized American British expatriates were no longer British subjects. And they saw an American seaman, once impressed, as a new British subject. That was just the way that it was. No one could be sure of who was who, and who belonged where.

All of this was occurring at the same time that American attitudes toward the British were seemingly ambivalent. The Britishisms of the colonists hadn't disappeared after the Revolutionary War. British ships appeared in American harbors and shipyards for provisioning and repair. Even the Declaration of Independence referred to "the ties of our common kindred." One political strain of the time urged rapprochement with Great Britain as a natural and economically necessary development.

It was into this world without boundaries that the USS *Chesapeake* set sail on June 22, 1807, and before she had gotten very far out to sea, everything would change. The adolescent America, successfully separated from its parent Great Britain, would take the first steps into adulthood as a sovereign nation with a powerful navy.

Whether ripped from the bosoms of their families by men in top hats, or grabbed on the docks by thugs with cudgels, victims of the press gangs had little recourse but to accept their fates, walk the gangplanks and hope that they could eventually find their ways home. *The Mariners' Museum, Newport News, Virginia.*

Up until that day, the need for a U.S. Navy had been once again in question. After the Tripolitan War, fiscal prudence had led to a reduction in its standing forces. Some wanted to change its emphasis from large frigates on the world stage to more and smaller ships and gunboats in defense of American harbors. All arguments were quieted by what happened to the *Chesapeake* on a pleasant summer afternoon, as Commander James Barron sailed her up the Elizabeth River and out of Hampton Roads toward the Atlantic.

Barron had been born into a seafaring family in Hampton, Virginia, in 1768. His father was James Barron, a merchant seaman who had become commodore of the Virginia state navy of the Revolution, and his brother was Commodore Samuel Barron, who served in the navy from 1798 to 1810. The younger James Barron was tall and broad shouldered, and his nearsightedness likely led to what was deemed a comfortable and engaging face. He had commanded the USS *President* in the early part of the Tripolitan War, and then sailed the *Chesapeake* home from the Mediterranean in 1803. In 1807 he received orders to become commander of the Mediterranean forces and return the *Chesapeake*, as flagship, to Mediterranean service.

It was supposed to have been an uneventful cruise to Europe. Just as the *Chesapeake* had been the home to women and newborn infants in earlier years, she was now something of a passenger and freight ship. Among the passengers were a husband and wife, their three children and two servants headed off to administrative work in the Mediterranean, and an eleven-member Italian marine band heading home with all of their instruments. She was also taking supplies for other ships in the Mediterranean, including assorted furniture and a horse. "The business of coiling away her cables," wrote James Fenimore Cooper, "was still going on, while the cabin

Excerpted from the song "The Impressment of an American Sailor Boy," sung onboard the British prison ship *Crown Prince*, July 4, 1813

When sick at heart, with hope deferr'd,
  Kind sleep his wasting form embrac'd,
Some ready minion ply'd the lash,
  And the lov'd dream of freedom chac'd.

Fast to an end his miseries drew;
  The deadly hectic flush'd his cheek;
On his pale brow the cold dew hung,
  He sigh'd, and sunk upon the deck!

The sailor's woes drew forth no sigh;
  No hand would close the sailor's eye;
Remorseless, his pale corpse they gave
  Unshrouded, to the friendly wave.

And as he sunk beneath the tide,
  A hellish shout arose;
Exultingly the demons cried,
  "So fare all Albion's REBEL foes!"

bulk-head, cabin furniture, and some temporary pantries were all standing aft…the guns were all loaded and shotted, but on examination, it was found that there was a deficiency in rammers, wads, matches, gun-locks, and powder-horns."

Her crew of 381 was largely inexperienced, and 32 of them were sick. By order of the surgeon they languished in hammocks strung between the guns on the upper deck to gain benefit from the pleasant weather at sea.

It was not to be a pleasant journey, however. British forces had been lurking just off the Virginia Capes, and it was suspected that four of the *Chesapeake*'s crew were British subjects, deserters.

The *Norfolk Public Ledger* of June 24 produced an extensive narrative of what followed:

We are now to present to our readers the details of a most unexampled outrage, in the perpetration of which the blood

Commodore James Barron. *The Mariners' Museum, Newport News, Virginia.*

of our countrymen has been shed by the hand of violence, and the honor and independence of our nation insulted beyond the possibility of further forbearance.

At a very early hour yesterday morning a report reached this place which produced a degree of agitation beyond anything we ever witnessed or can attempt to describe.

After further paragraphs in a tone presaging the outrage that was about to rise from the young American nation, the *Ledger* reported on what had taken place between the USS *Chesapeake* and the HMS *Leopard.*

At 9 o'clock the Leopard, by signal from the Commodore's ship, had got under way and stood out to sea. About 3 o'clock the

NORFOLK GAZETTE And PUBLICK LEDGER

SINT HIC ETIAM SUA PRÆMIA LAUDI

Chesapeake and Leopard approached, when the customary signal of firing a gun to leeward, the signal for friends, was made from both ships. Being about 3 leagues from the land, the ships came within hail, when the commander of the Leopard hailed he hoped Commodore Barron was well, and informed him that he had dispatches for the Commodore.

The ships hove to, and a boat came on board the Chesapeake with a letter from [Leopard's] Captain Humphries. In this letter was a copy of one from Admiral Berkley at Halifax, to all the British commanders on this station, in which they were ordered to demand from the commander of the Chesapeake four British seamen named in the letter, and that if they were not delivered by fair means to use force…Commodore Barron returned an answer to this letter, in which he stated that orders of his Government forbade him to permit his vessel be searched or to deliver a man from her. The boat from the Leopard had no sooner returned onboard than a gun from her was fired ahead of the Chesapeake, and instantly followed by a broad-side from the Leopard, accompanied by swivels and small arms. Six other broadsides followed—the two ships then within pistol shot.

On board the Chesapeake all was astonishment. The ship was unprepared for action, no man at his quarters, and some of the officers at dinner. In this situation Commodore Barron hailed the Leopard repeatedly without effect; he then ordered the colours to be struck; as this was doing, a gun from the Chesapeake was fired, upon which the Leopard responded with another broadside. The colours being now down an officer was dispatched to the Chesapeake, who on coming on board expressed some regret on behalf of his commander for what had happened. He was received with great indignation by the American officers, who tendered their swords, which he refused, saying that he wanted the four men and nothing more, and demanded the muster role, which was produced by the Purser, and then was exhibited the degrading spectacle of nearly four hundred Americans mustered on the deck of an American man-of-war by order of a British lieutenant, and four of the crew taken away.

The *Leopard* brings orders to the *Chesapeake* to give up four named British seamen in its crew under direction of the British commander in North America that if the *Chesapeake* was found, it was to be searched for deserters. *The Mariners' Museum, Newport News, Virginia.*

In reporting that spoke of three casualties of the encounter (a fourth would come later), and went on for hundreds of words, the article stated, "It is impossible that on such an occasion, there can be but one sentiment in the heart of every American. The independence of our country has been attacked, and in defending it our fellow citizens have been killed. Submission to the demand made on Commodore Barron could not have been made without relinquishing our right as an independent nation."

The British attack had arisen out of a frustration. Every one of its vessels in the region had lost crew members that year. Seamen most

The *Leopard* devastates the *Chesapeake* at close range. In keeping with the customs of the time, the *Chesapeake* lowered her flag and Commodore Barron prepared to surrender his ship to Captain Salisbury Pryce Humphreys of the *Leopard*. The offer would figure in Barron's later court-martial. Humphreys refused to take the *Chesapeake* prize, offered whatever assistance was needed, deplored the loss of life and sailed away to rejoin his squadron. *Wilson History Room, Portsmouth (Virginia) Public Library.*

presumed to be potential deserters were not allowed on shore, but many dove overboard and made the long swim, or commandeered small boats to reach Norfolk, Portsmouth, Hampton or Newport News, where they could find work in U.S. naval and commercial shipping. It would take more than a hundred years of the deliberations of naval historians to determine, however, the true nature of the four men taken from the *Chesapeake* (and that many of the crew were, indeed, British deserters). They can all be named, and the biographies of three of them were given in James Barron's papers after the assault. William Ware was a native American, born in Frederick County, Maryland. "He is an Indian looking man," wrote Barron, and in a supporting affidavit Barron asserted that he was a former slave. Daniel Martin was a native of Westport, Massachusetts. "He is a coloured man." J. Strachan was born in Queen Anne's County, Maryland. "He is a white man about 5 feet 7 inches tall." They were all American born, but the problem was that in the topsy-turvy world of impressments, desertions and vague citizenships, they may or may not have once been British sailors. The three were imprisoned, but the fourth, Jenkin Ratford, actually an Englishman, was publicly hanged in Halifax as an example.

As described by the *Ledger*, the attack upon the *Chesapeake* resulted in an explosion of outrage. Almost as soon as the ship had limped back to the Gosport Shipyard, severely damaged and embarrassed, crowds were gathering in the streets of Norfolk. Public officials were declaiming indignation and the promise of revenge. In England, the British foreign secretary sent a message to American Ambassador James Monroe referring to the "transaction" between the two ships

WASHINGTON CITY, June 26.

BRITISH OUTRAGE.

We give the publick the particulars of the following outrage on the American flag, under the influence of feelings, which, we are certain, are in unison with those entertained universally by our fellow citizens—feelings which cannot, which ought not to be suppressed. We know not, indeed, that this savage outrage has a precedent in naval annals.

On Monday last the United States frigate Chesapeake, of 38 guns, left the Capes, where there lay at anchor a British squadron consisting of three two-deckers and one frigate of 36 guns. As she passed this squadron without molestation, one of the two-deckers, the Leopard, put off, and went to sea before the Chesapeake. When the latter came up with the Leopard, at the distance of about three leagues from the squadron, her commander, captain Humphries, hailed the Chesapeake, and said he had a dispatch to deliver from the British commander in chief (meaning admiral Berkley, of the American station.) Commodore Barron, supposing it was a dispatch for Europe, hove to, when capt. Humphries sent on board of her a letter, covering an order of admiral Berkley, to take from the Chesapeake three men, alledged to be deserters from the Melampus frigate, and designating them by name. Commodore Barron replied by letter that no such men, as named in admiral Berkley's order, were on board, and added that his crew could not be mustered for examination by any other officers than his own. This answer was couched in terms of politeness. It was no sooner received than a broadside was discharged from the Leopard. The crew of the Chesapeake were at this time not at quarters, considering the Leopard a friend, and commodore Barron not contemplating the possibility of danger so immediately after leaving the Capes. No other attempt was therefore made to fight her than the discharge of a few straggling guns, while the Leopard repeated three or four more broadsides, when the Chesapeake struck her colours, after having three men killed and eighteen wounded.

A boat was then put off from the Leopard, with an officer, who demanded four men. Commodore Barron said he considered the Chesapeake a prize to the Leopard—the captain of which vessel said, no —that his orders were to take out the men, which, having executed, he had nothing further to do with her. Thus dismissed, she returned to Hampton Roads, where she now lies. She received in her hull 22 round shot, her fore-mast and main-mast destroyed, her mizen-mast greatly injured, and her standing rigging and sails very much cut.

Of the wounded 8 are considered dangerous, and two have lost an arm each. Commodore Barron suffered a contusion, received from a splinter, which is not serious. No other officer is wounded, excepting midshipman Broom, and he but slightly.

Nothing evinces in more striking colours the insolence of capt. Humphreys, than his immediate return, after this outrage, to the Capes, where he now lies with the other ships of the squadron.

National Intelligencer.

and expressing the "sincere concern and sorrow" of His Majesty's government. Monroe furiously replied, calling the event a "flagrant abuse," demanding that "the Officer who is responsible for it, shall suffer the punishment which so unexampled an aggression on the sovereignty of a Neutral nation justly deserves."

President Jefferson ordered all British ships in American waters "immediately and without any delay to depart from same." All communication and commerce with those ships and crews was to cease, and any American who did not comply with the order was to be punished.

But it was the public response that seemed to arouse a sense of nationalism perhaps not seen since the Revolutionary War. Near riots broke out, in the course of which some British water casks were broken, notable only because the British government formally asked for monetary compensation for their loss, a request more than informally denied.

The fourth casualty of the encounter was realized at the Marine Hospital (Portsmouth Naval Hospital) on June 24, 1807, in the name of Robert Macdonald. Reported the *Herald*, "The body was brought over from the Hospital Point, attended by a procession of boats to the market wharf. Minute guns from the artillery firing during the time, all the American shipping with colours at half mast." Four thousand citizens were in attendance.

The Calendar of State Papers of Virginia records the resolution of a public meeting held in Norfolk on June 25. It took on the tone and cadence of the Declaration of Independence.

And whereas we as individuals seriously deprecate the horrors of war and view it as one of the greatest evils which can befall our country, but when we behold our Fellow-Citizens impressed and forced by a tyrannical and arbitrary power to fight against their own country, and basely and insidiously murdered on our coasts, it becomes necessary, at this awful crisis to be prepared to meet the consequences which such conduct and such inclinations to give reasonable cause to expect—to discipline ourselves and be in readiness to take up arms in defense of those sacred rights which our forefathers purchased with their blood, and until our Government shall have been informed of the late glaring violation of our rights and our sovereignty in the unwarrantable and unprovoked attack upon the United States Frigate Chesapeake…therefore…

The "therefores" were numerous, and included calling upon the mayor of Norfolk to create a militia, and the citizens of Hampton Roads to wear crape for ten days in respect to those lost on the *Chesapeake*. It asked that a committee be formed to go beyond the precincts of the city to inform the citizenry of the sea coast as to what had happened and encourage the expression of similar public outrage, which was immediately returned.

The citizens of Williamsburg recommended that British seamen seized in Norfolk be held hostage against the safe return of the *Chesapeake* sailors. Citizens of the Richmond vicinity sent a letter to President Jefferson noting America's peaceable nature, but "when we recollect, on the other hand, the innumerable insults and aggressions which Great Britain has inflicted on our just and lawful commerce; we can only discover in this recent act of violence the consummation of a system which has for its object the prostration of neutral rights, at the feet of a haughty and ambitious power. The door of negotiation is finally closed; the first blow of war has been struck."

The outrage spread. It was the Resolution of the Citizens of Franklin, Kentucky, dated July 24, that the event seemed to be "a settled determination of the British government to avail herself of her naval superiority to depredate on the property, to harass the citizens, destroy the commerce, and insult the independence of the United States of America." It went on to list other examples of British arrogance, and put down in Resolution number 5 "our opinion and firm hope, that if we are to lose our independence, it shall be lost with swords in our hands." The Citizens of the First Congressional District of Pennsylvania declared the attack on the *Chesapeake* "an act of such consummate violence and wrong, and of so barbarous and murderous a character that it would debase and degrade any nation and much more so a nation of freemen to submit to it."

Anger spread, too, to Commodore James Barron, and it began with a letter to the secretary of the navy from six officers of the *Chesapeake* dated the day after the event. It decried "the premature surrender of the United States ship *Chesapeake* of 40 guns to the English ship-of-war *Leopard* of 50 guns without their previous knowledge or consent." It went on to say that they (the undersigned)

are compelled by imperious duty, by the honour of their flag, by the honour of their countrymen and by all that is dear to themselves. To request that an order may be issued for the arrest

of Commodore James Barron on the charges herewith exhibited
which the undersigned pledge themselves to prove true, viz.
1ˢᵗ. On the probability of an engagement, for neglecting to clear
his ship for action.
2ndly. For not doing his utmost to take or destroy a vessel which
we conceived it his duty to have done.

Navy Secretary Robert Smith was inclined to agree. He had already directed that the wounded ship be put under the command of the naval hero Stephen Decatur, and that the process begin toward a court-martial proceeding in the matter. In a letter to the editor of the *Ledger* of August 3, 1807, James Barron brushed off the accusations flying around him "as a court of enquiry will shortly convene for the purpose of investigating the affair of the *Chesapeake* and *Leopard*, and through that channel the publick may expect a correct knowledge of facts." Barron did, however, take another occasion to call his officers "the greatest cowards that ever stood on a ship's deck."

An editorial in the *Ledger* a few days later took Barron's side, and, picking up on a popular perception that Thomas Jefferson was soft on national defense, suggested that a coverup of the facts was taking place and the people were not being given full information. The editorial demanded that the truth be arrived at quickly, and the *Chesapeake* be put back on line with dispatch. "As we have but *very few* frigates, the people of the United States feel a great interest in the fate of those few, particularly as we have no prospect of ever getting anymore, during the life of Mr. Jefferson or his politicks."

The court-martial was held onboard the embattled ship. Among those who sat in judgment of James Barron were Stephen Decatur and James Lawrence who would, himself, lead the *Chesapeake* into an even more decisive battle with the British five years later. Barron was cleared of three charges against him, but one remained: "neglecting on the probability of an engagement, to clear the ship for action." Barron was given a five-year suspension from the navy without pay.

The results of the meeting between the two ships would reverberate for years. Her new captain, Stephen Decatur, would contribute to the centuries of a damned reputation for the *Chesapeake* by calling her a ship without honor. At the same time, he brought her to the status of a ship ready to respond immediately to any challenge, prepared to blow the *Leopard* out of the water if the two should meet again.

The Commodore Theatre (right) beside the graveyard of the Trinity Church in Portsmouth, Virginia, which contains the grave of Commodore James Barron (below). The theatre was built in 1945. Still in use, it has been declared a Virginia Historic Landmark, and is listed on the National Register of Historic Places. Unseen behind Barron's grave are the gravestones of two of his grandchildren, both passed away before the age of fifteen. *Kirn Library, Norfolk, Sargeant Memorial Room.*

James Barron banished himself for many years to Copenhagen, where he lived in a small garret, developed his hobby as an inventor into salable products and became a leader of the American expatriate community. When, at last, he felt it was time to return home, he didn't have sufficient funds for the journey. He was vindicated to a degree by the British themselves, when in 1811 they declared the attack to have been in error, "an unauthorized act of the officer in command of His Majesty's forces on the coast of America." Many duels were said to have broken out between quarreling principals over the following years, culminating in a duel that would end an era.

At the time of James Barron's court-martial, Stephen Decatur had petitioned Navy Secretary Smith to be excused from the panel, admitting to his distaste and lack of respect for the commodore. His petition denied, he was among the most critical of Barron in the court's judgment. In the face of Barron's shame, Decatur would continue to distinguish himself in service of the navy, though he would lose the frigate *President* to the British after driving her aground in a January snowstorm in 1815. At a dinner held in his honor in Norfolk in 1816, he offered a toast that has been paraphrased in modern times: "Our country! In her intercourse with foreign nations, may she always be in the right, and always successful, right or wrong."

But Stephen Decatur would not let up on James Barron. When the commodore returned from Europe to seek engagement with the navy once again, it was Decatur who most stood in his way, and it became Barron who proposed a duel between the two. Decatur, who had a long and sometimes troubled history with duels, accepted the challenge. The two met on a field in Bladensburg, Maryland, on March 22, 1820. It would be the last day in the life of Stephen Decatur Jr. And as he lay dying, the wounded Barron would utter, "God bless you, Decatur."

"Farewell, farewell, Barron," Decatur replied.

Commodore James Barron would be reinstated to naval service, spend some years himself as commander of the Gosport Shipyard and die in 1851. He is buried in the Trinity Churchyard of Portsmouth, Virginia, right next door to the Commodore movie and dinner theatre.

The political and policy result of the attack upon the USS *Chesapeake* by the HMS *Leopard* was more measured than the angry oaths of American citizens, or the theatre of duels and recriminations. At first, American militia was placed on guard against certain subsequent attacks by the British, especially one that might come against New York City. Some who were previously of a more peaceable mind in the American government began to think more defensively, but the following years would see continued debate and disagreement as to the nature and use of ships by the U.S. Navy: Should they be in ordinary or in action? Should they be large or small? Should they operate independently or in fleets?

A long-simmering debate about the righteousness of the Barron-Decatur duel extended into the *Washington Post* of March 1957. Responding to a previous article critical of Barron, Ronald May, Washington correspondent for the Madison, Wisconsin *Capital Times*, suggested in an op-ed another insight into the enmity between the two men. Decatur had married Susan Wheeler, the illegitimate daughter of Norfolk Mayor Luke Wheeler, in 1808. "Susan was a wild sort whom her father could not control. She was beautiful, vivacious, intelligent and uninhibited…The proper Barron was shocked to learn that Decatur had married Susan, and told him so. There is evidence that Decatur made a crack that Barron, who was married, had designs on her himself."

There were no more attacks by the British, though their ships continued to menace American trade in Europe and the unchartable world of impressments and desertions continued as the Napoleonic Wars kept up their demands on the Royal Navy. American embargoes and trade restrictions that might have made the British more civilized in this regard failed miserably. In 1811, an exchange occurred that seemed to mirror the *Chesapeake/Leopard* affair and offered a small sense of American revenge for that attack. In the campaign against impressments, the USS *President* tracked down and clashed with a smaller British ship, the *Little Belt*, killing nine and wounding twenty-three others. It could not be clear who fired first, and the British accused the *President* of unprovoked aggression. The *London Courier* declaimed that "the blood of our murdered countrymen must be revenged."

And so it went in the years after the *Leopard* attacked the *Chesapeake* in 1807. By a strict reading of the papers and documents of history there is no connection between the attack on the American frigate and the war between the two nations that would follow five years later. The matter was resolved legally between them in 1811, with reparations from England and the release of the two Americans originally taken who were still alive in Halifax.

But in a broader view, what happened to the USS *Chesapeake* in 1807—an attack eventually deemed to have occurred in error—would set the path toward a war that would begin because of a missed communication five years later. And it would hasten the end of the first chapter of the *Chesapeake*'s journey.

CHAPTER 3

A FUNERAL IN HALIFAX

When Stephen Decatur regained destructive possession of the USS *Philadelphia* off Tripoli, his second in command was Lieutenant James Lawrence. They had led their band of sailors through days of privation on an old merchant ship, been tossed about by the sea, deceived the guardians of the *Philadelphia/Gift of Allah* and fought their way onto the ship without a casualty. In James Fenimore Cooper's telling of it, Lieutenant Lawrence moved quickly to the berth deck and forward storerooms of the ship and set them afire.

This was not what James Lawrence was supposed to do with his life. He was supposed to become a lawyer, as was his father, John Lawrence, before him, and his brother, too.

John Lawrence of New Jersey had been accused of being a British Loyalist during the Revolutionary War. He was acquitted of that charge, and eventually became mayor of Burlington, where James was born at what is now 459 High Street on October 1, 1781. He was the youngest of eleven children, and when his mother died soon after his birth he came under the care of two older sisters, a circumstance that history points to as an influence on the compassionate man he would become.

As it pertained to the sea, the world that Lawrence was born into was a very small one. James Barron had been the son of John and brother of Samuel Barron, both naval captains. James Barron, years before the fateful duel, had been an instructor to the young Stephen Decatur Jr., son of naval commander Stephen Decatur Sr. James Lawrence would serve with Decatur at the court-martial of James Barron, and all three would be commander of the USS *Chesapeake* at one point or another. The exploits of all of them would be described by the young nation's first popular naval historian, James Fenimore Cooper. Cooper had also been born in Burlington, New Jersey, on September 15, 1789, at 457 High Street—an attached house next door to James Lawrence's first home. Though their lives would cross paths repeatedly, Lawrence and Cooper did not grow up together. They were both gentle, principled and willful young men, each with a determination to live his life by his own lights.

Cooper was the great-great-grandson of James Cooper, who had come from Stratford-on-Avon, England, in 1679, a Quaker who spent his life acquiring large parcels of land in New York and New Jersey. The young James Cooper's mother, Elizabeth, was the daughter of Richard Fenimore, who had arrived in America from Oxfordshire, England. His father William, a judge and former congressman, would found the town of Cooperstown, New York. It was there in the territory of Otsego Lake, and the Susquehanna River headwaters of the Chesapeake Bay, where James gained the knowledge of nature and Indians that would inform much of his writing. He attended Yale University in 1803, but paid more attention to the surrounding woods and the shores of Long Island Sound than to the classroom. By his third year at Yale he had become so noncompliant with academic restraints that he was expelled from the school.

His father thought that a naval career might be better suited to the boy's temperament, and young James Fenimore Cooper joined the Merchant Marine, a common steppingstone to receiving a commission in the United States Navy. His first journey took forty tempestuous days, crossing the Atlantic with a cargo of flour, and he arrived a committed sailor. In London, however, he gained the experience of dealing with the press gangs as they roamed the docks looking for labor. In a continuation of his journey into the Mediterranean, his ship was nearly captured by pirates, and as she finally sailed back home across the ocean she came in contact

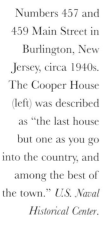

Numbers 457 and 459 Main Street in Burlington, New Jersey, circa 1940s. The Cooper House (left) was described as "the last house but one as you go into the country, and among the best of the town." *U.S. Naval Historical Center.*

with an English brig whose captain gave the Americans their first knowledge of the *Leopard*'s attack upon the *Chesapeake*. James returned home with a distinct dislike of the British.

Later in his life, James Fenimore Cooper wrote *Ned Myers; or, A Life Before the Mast*, an oral history of one of the shipmates of his youth. The book ranges all over the world, and its passing reference to the fate of the *Chesapeake* mirrored Cooper's experience.

> *When near the American coast, we spoke an English brig that gave us an account of the affair between the "Leopard" and the "Chesapeake," though he made his own countrymen come out second-best. Bitter were the revilings of Mr. Irish when the pilot told us the real state of the case. As was usual with this ship's luck, we tided it up the bay and river, and got safe alongside of the wharf at Philadelphia, at last. Here our crew was broken up, of course, and with the exception of Jack Pugh, my brother apprentice, and Cooper, I never saw a single soul of them afterwards. Most of them went on to New York, and were swallowed up in the great vortex of seamen. Mr. Irish, I heard, died the next voyage he made, chief mate of an Indiaman.*

As expected, Cooper became a navy midshipman, and history records that his tenure in the navy, though short, was distinguished. It was spent mostly on the Great Lakes, and for a time under the command of James Lawrence, who kept meticulous records. For Cooper's service on the USS *Wasp*, Lawrence noted, he had served

An undated, but believed to be a childhood sketch titled *The Light Horse of Philadelphia*, signed by James Lawrence. The Philadelphia Light Horse was a group of prominent men who, in 1774, formed themselves into a military unit in service to the Continental Congress and General George Washington. Its name was later changed to First Troop Philadelphia City Cavalry, and it served in support of U.S. military efforts worldwide into the twenty-first century. *Gloucester County Historical Society, New Jersey.*

for six months and thirteen days at a pay of $19.00 per month. He had been overpaid for that service by $26.40 once the Hospital Fund payment of $1.22 was subtracted. Among his last assignments was the creation of a recruiting station near South Street in Manhattan. He left the navy in May of 1810, returned the overpayment and went on to become one of America's most famous writers.

By the age of twelve, James Lawrence knew that he wanted to go to sea. His father wanted him to go to law school, however, and so he set out on that course, starting at Woodbury Academy, which Stephen Decatur Jr. had previously attended. He continued studies under his older brother, John Lawrence, Esq., all the while keeping his eye on the nearby Delaware River and the path it took down to the Atlantic. At age fifteen, fortuitously or not, his father passed on, and James was released from the prospect of a life in the courts. Back in Burlington, he studied navigation under the noted academic and scientist John Griscom, after which he was accepted into the navy as a midshipman in September 1798.

The era of British-American relations that was kick-started by the *Leopard*'s attack on the *Chesapeake* in 1807 came to a head five years later for want of a yet-to-be-invented telegraph. Though Britain had essentially apologized for the attack and made reparations in 1811, its conduct over those years was little changed. Impressment was still a problem, driven by the manpower needs of the continuing war between Britain and France. Both countries continued to interfere with the trade of neutral nations, including America. In Britain, that interference was codified under the *Orders in Council* that restricted trade with France by neutrals. The attack on the American *Chesapeake*, and the reverse attack on the British *Little Belt*, had been but two of a number of skirmishes between the two navies.

The Americans were not blameless. On land, continuing American expansion into its northwest—now Ohio, Michigan and Illinois—pushed up against native populations whose allegiances lay with the British, and when they fought back the British were blamed for their actions. Out of the Indian uprisings came the great chief Tecumseh, a charismatic orator and warrior who would give his name to Tecumseh's War over a territory between what are now, at each point of the compass, Toledo, Ohio; Vincennes, Indiana; Chicago, Illinois; and Grand Rapids, Michigan. Like the *Chesapeake/Leopard* affair, Tecumseh's War was presumed to be settled in 1811, but it would lead naturally into the larger war that followed.

Things were further confused by the matter of Canada's identity. Upper Canada, now essentially all of modern Ontario, held a population of British Loyalists from the Revolutionary War and later arriving people with mixed loyalties. It was a natural leap for some American politicians to think that a war with Great Britain might offer opportunities for expansion into Canada. The British held a firmer hand in Lower Canada, now essentially eastern Quebec and north to Newfoundland. Halifax, Nova Scotia, had become the powerful British headquarters of the North American East Coast.

In 1811, the British, worried about the prospect of fighting a war on two fronts, began to take a less belligerent tone with America. The settlement of the *Chesapeake/Leopard* affair was a first step, but it did not occur soon enough for most Americans. It was followed by orders down the line to avoid sea skirmishes as possible, and to sail clear of the American coast. Then an offer was made to suspend the *Orders in Council*, but with conditions unacceptable to President James Madison.

Given the technologies and tensions of the times, communication across the Atlantic had often worked remarkably well. Belligerents

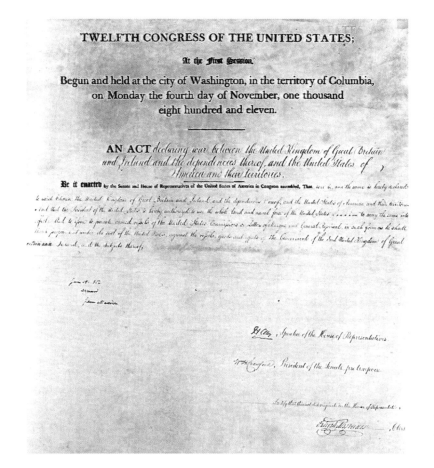

"An Act declaring war between the United Kingdom of Great Britain and Ireland and the dependencies thereof and the United States of America and their territories. Approved June 18, 1812 by James Madison. *U.S. National Archives.*"

were generally able to deal with each other in a businesslike way, and there was a sort of honor system about communications in place among captains of the sea, but any message still took as long as the winds would dictate to get from point A to point B. Thus, on June 16, 1812, the British announced the complete suspension of the *Orders in Council*, but two days later, having no knowledge of the fact, the Americans declared war on the British. American leadership later suggested that the war might have been averted had they only known. But it was too late, and the War of 1812 was begun. It would go on for less than three years, and end inconclusively. Its chief accomplishments would be the strengthening of American sovereignty and naval power.

Ships of the Line
Moving fortresses that could give and receive heavy firepower and could move quickly and in concert with others in the line of battle.

The war was fought on land, the Great Lakes and the Atlantic Ocean. At its outset the navy was not prepared to fight it, though its efforts would result in a spectacular year. Not including a fleet of ineffectual gunboats, its forces included just sixteen vessels with five hundred guns between them. The British had more than six hundred vessels, a quarter of them ships of the line, but they were preoccupied with the European wars and the British hoped that the Americans might un-declare the war when they learned that the *Orders in Council* had been rescinded. That was not to be, and the small American navy got a jump-start on things by eventually determining to seek out and destroy any British ship found in its waters, one on one.

On August 19, 1812, the USS *Constitution*, captained by Isaac Hull, destroyed the HMS *Guerriere* in fifteen minutes of intense fire four hundred miles southeast of Halifax. British cannonballs seemed only to bounce off the white oak sides of the *Constitution*, giving her the nickname "Old Ironsides." On October 18 the sloop of war *Wasp*, captained by Jacob Jones, took His Majesty's frig *Frolic* in a gale off Cape Hatteras, North Carolina, though victor and prize were captured by the British the next day and taken to Bermuda. Also in October the USS *United States*, captained by Stephen Decatur, took the HMS *Macedonian* five hundred miles south of the Azores and had her flag sent to the White House, where it was received by First Lady Dolly Madison as the nation cheered. In December the *Constitution*, now under Commodore William Bainbridge, took the frigate *Java* off the coast of Brazil, and in February the *Hornet*, under Master Commandant James Lawrence, took the *Peacock* off northern South America. The *Peacock* sank swiftly, and Lawrence would later be remembered for his kindness to her surviving crew. The USS *Chesapeake*, captained by Samuel Evans, a former commandant of the Gosport Shipyard, patrolled from Africa to the West Indies. She saw no confrontation with British naval ships, but took five merchant ships as prize.

The American response to these successes contained no little measure of surprise. Even the secretary of the navy, Paul Hamilton, had written that, though American sailors were superior, "when I reflect on the overwhelming force of our enemy, my heart swells almost to bursting, and all the consolation I have is that in falling, they will fall nobly."

The British response to these events carried every measure of surprise. The *London Times* of March 20, 1813, reported,

> *Any one who would have predicted such a result of an American war this time last year would have been treated as a madman or a traitor. He would have been told, if his opponents had condescended to argue with him, that long ere seven months had elapsed the American flag would have been swept from the seas, the contemptible navy of the United States annihilated, and their marine arsenals rendered a heap of ruins.*

In the spirit of that anger, the British finally began to turn the war in the Atlantic in their favor by enlarging a blockade of the East Coast that proved to be effective in limiting the movement of American ships. One of the ships enforcing the blockade was the HMS *Shannon.*

In summer 1812 the USS *Constitution* found herself surrounded by enemy vessels off the coast of New Jersey on a windless sea. As the British closed in over sixty hours, she was saved by kedging, a process in which sailors rowed two hundred yards ahead of the ship and dropped an anchor. The capstan was used to pull the ship two hundred yards forward. *The Mariners' Museum, Newport News, Virginia.*

The gun deck of a typical U.S. Navy frigate. *Naval Shipyard Museum, Portsmouth, Virginia.*

Admiral Sir Philip Bowes Vere Broke ran the *Shannon* like a fine Swiss watch, ready to spring into battle with full force at the mere tick of a second hand. Broke was born in Suffolk, England, in 1776, trained in the Portsmouth Dockyards, rose in skill and esteem through the European Wars and was made commander of the *Shannon* in August 1806. Even American historians of the U.S. Naval Center avow that he had "made *Shannon* into one of the finest gunnery ships in the Royal Navy, and probably in the World."

Broke's second in command on the *Shannon* was Lieutenant Provo Wallis of Halifax. His father had been chief clerk of the Halifax Shipyard at a time when seniority was everything in the British navy. A day's difference in tenure could mean the difference between commanding a ship or not; thus, his father put him on the muster roll of the HMS *L'Oiseau* as an able-bodied seaman just a few days short of his fourth birthday. By the time he completed his schooling and entered service at Portsmouth, he had ten years of seniority. He would be on the naval payroll for ninety-six years in all. And, like P.B.V. Broke, his spark of enduring fame would be given to him by the USS *Chesapeake*.

In April of 1813, the *Chesapeake* came to the end of her first successful cruise of the war with her arrival in Boston Harbor. Captain Samuel Evans wrote a report to Commodore Stephen Decatur recounting the events of the cruise, and noted needed repairs. "The ship will require a new Main Mast," he said, "the one in being decay'd and in working in yesterday a heavy flaw carried away the Main topmast by which we unfortunately lost three men, and Sprung the head of the Mizen Mast which I expect will have to be replac'd likewise." Decatur replied with an urging that, in the name of time and expense, he find a way to repair, rather than replace, the masts, and chided him for previous excesses. "The last equipment of the *Chesapeake*," wrote Decatur, "was in many respects, highly extravagant; particularly for the luxurious indulgence of the fancy of her commander and officers, much of which will never be allowed by this department."

Evans was tired and was plagued by a recurring problem with a war wound to his left eye. Decatur's words may have put him over the edge, and he requested shore duty. James Lawrence was chosen to replace him in command of the *Chesapeake*, an assignment that Lawrence did not want. The *Constitution* was in the shipyard and the extra months it would take to reequip her for service would allow him, if he were her captain, to take care of his sick wife. Upon arriving on the *Chesapeake* in May of 1813, he found a crew made hostile by bureaucratic failures in the awarding of earned prize money, and advanced some of his own funds to solve the matter. The officer corps onboard the ship was young and inexperienced; the first lieutenant, August Ludlow, was just twenty-one years of age. The idea that the *Chesapeake* was an unlucky ship remained as an undercurrent to everything else.

The ship was given the mission of getting out to sea for a cruise off the Gulf of St. Lawrence to intercept supplies and reinforcements headed for Canada. The *Shannon* lay just outside the harbor as a blockade, but she was alone and the two ships were about evenly matched as fighting frigates. The *Chesapeake* had a larger crew, 381 to the *Shannon*'s 330, but the British crew was perhaps the most highly trained of both navies. Lawrence measured the odds and decided to head for the sea, engaging the *Shannon* if necessary. He did not know that, in another of those missed communications that may have changed the course of history, Broke had already issued him a challenge, undelivered by the time the *Chesapeake* set sail on the first day of June.

Its language was in keeping with the exquisite courtesy exchanged by naval captains of opposing forces in those days. "Sir," it began. "As the *Chesapeake* appears now ready for Sea, I request you will do me the favor to meet the *Shannon* with her, Ship to Ship, to try the fortune of our respective flags." It went on to discuss at length the current readiness of the *Shannon* in specific terms, referred to erroneous reporting of her crew size in the Boston newspapers, assured Lawrence that other British ships would not be involved and concluded:

James Lawrence. An engraving after a painting by Alonzo Chappell. *U.S. Naval Historical Center.*

You will feel it as a compliment if I say that the result of our meeting may be the most grateful service I can render to my country; and I doubt not, that you, equally confident of success, will feel convinced that it is only by repeated triumphs, in even combats, that your little navy can now hope to console your country for the loss of that trade it can no longer protect. Favour me with a speedy reply.

We are short of provisions and water, and cannot stay long here.

I have the honour to be, sir,
Your obedient, humble servant,
P.B.V. BROKE,
Captain of H.B.M. ship Shannon.

Also included in the challenge that Lawrence never received was the offer from Broke to let the *Chesapeake* choose virtually any time and place for the encounter, which, had Lawrence known about it, might have given him more time and space to get his ship and crew better prepared and positioned for battle. Instead, the *Chesapeake* headed out of Boston Harbor knowing that she would probably have to fight the *Shannon*, and with the confidence that she could succeed in an immediate encounter. That confidence extended to the people of Boston, who cheered it from the shores as she got underway. Victory dinners were already being planned for the *Chesapeake*'s safe return that evening.

The battle that actually took place was no more than fifteen minutes long, and still resounds in the history of naval warfare. It was first reported in the newspapers of England (not reaching the *London Gazette* until forty days after the event) and America in speculation and with some error. Later historians would quibble over fine points. James Fenimore Cooper would write about it extensively, of course. In Teddy Roosevelt's *The Naval War of 1812*, published a year after he became president, Roosevelt would critique Cooper's work:

Cooper, with his usual cheerful optimism, says that the incidents of the battle, excepting its short duration, are "altogether the results of the chances of war," and that it was mainly decided by "fortuitous events as unconnected with any particular merit on the one side as they are with any particular demerit on the other." Most naval men consider it a species of treason to regard the defeat as due to anything but extraordinary ill fortune. And yet no disinterested reader can help acknowledging that Hard as it is to breathe a word against such a man as Lawrence, a very Bayard of the seas, who was admired as much for his dauntless bravery as he was loved for his gentleness and uprightness, it must be confessed that he acted rashly.

Discussion and debate about the battle continues into the twenty-first century, much of it only comprehensible to those who have an acute understanding of the physics and architecture of sailing battleships. The most accessible writing about the encounter was published in 1866 by Broke's biographer, the Reverend J.D. Brighton, excerpted here.

The Setting

The morning of that most eventful day, Tuesday June 1st, 1813, broke over the shores and islands of the Bay of Boston in unclouded summer loveliness. A faint breeze rippled the waters, and the rising sun cast long rays of light and broken brilliancy over the wide and gently-heaving bosom of Boston Bay. The Shannon, under easy sail, slowly floated down the eastern coast

This painting of the battle between the *Shannon* and *Chesapeake*, though dramatic, is probably not accurate. Varying accounts place the battle between fifteen and thirty miles from Boston Light, pictured at left. *U.S. Naval Historical Center.*

in order to take an early look into the harbour and upon the vessels of the enemy. Viewed from seaward, a more peaceful scene could scarcely be conceived. The lighthouse, friendly alike to friend and foe, the distant shore—the light hazy clouds over the port and town of Boston—and the lofty masts and wide-spread spars of the man-of-war lying ready for sea—these, as usual, were the prominent objects on which the eager and anxious gaze of Broke had often before rested. But to-day, or at farthest to-morrow, he had strong hopes the issue would be decided.

The Approach

…The word passed on lightening wings along the decks—"She is coming out," and soon every Shannon's eye was on her movements. At length the watch and ward of weary, toilsome weeks was ended. Sail after sail spread forth, flag after flag unfurled, and with all the speed the light air and ebbing tide could yield her, and attended by a large number of lesser craft to witness and applaud her expected triumph, the haughty Chesapeake bore down upon her waiting adversary. Her commander, Lawrence, glowing with recent triumph, anticipated an easy victory. Colossal in figure, and with muscular power superior to most men, he was on this day fatally conspicuous by the white vest and other habiliments he had assumed.

The reference is to a criticism of Lawrence that, already a very tall man at six feet, four inches, he made himself further visible to any British shooter by wearing resplendent clothing and a tall hat.

Broke's Charge

"Shannon's! You know that, from various causes, the Americans have lately triumphed, on several occasions, over the British lag in our frigates. This will not daunt you, since you know the truth, that disparity of force was the chief reason. But they have gone farther: they have said, and they have published it in their papers, that the English have forgotten the way to fight. You will let them know to-day there are Englishmen in the Shannon who still know how to fight. Don't try to dismast her. Fire into her quarters; main deck into main deck; quarterdeck into quarterdeck. Kill the men and the ship is yours. Don't hit them about the head, for they have steel caps on, but give it them through the body. Don't cheer. Go quietly to your quarters. I feel sure you will all do your duty; and remember, you now have the blood of hundreds of your countrymen to avenge!"

The First Broadsides

The ships were closing fast. The sails of the Chesapeake came rapidly between the slanting rays of the evening sun and the Shannon, darkening the main deck ports of the latter, whilst the increasing ripple of the water against her bow as she approached could be distinctly heard at all the guns of the after battery on the Shannon's silent main deck. In another moment, the desired position being attained, the Shannon commenced the action by firing her after or fourteenth main-deck gun; the steady old captain of the gun, Billy Mindham (Captain Broke's faithful coxswain), having first reported to the officer of his quarters, Lieut. Wallis, that his gun bore, and received permission to fire; a second afterwards, her after carronade on the quarterdeck; then her thirteenth main deck gun; and, as the Chesapeake ranged alongside, she received, in close and steady succession, the whole of the broadside. The effect of this (as witnessed from the Shannon's tops) was truly withering. A hurricane of shot, splinters, torn hammocks, cut rigging, and wreck of every kind, was hurled like a cloud across the deck. Of 150 men quartered thereon, more than 100 were instantly laid low. Nor was this all. In this moment of deadly strife, Lawrence, who

The *Shannon* commences the battle with the *Chesapeake*. Painted by J.C. Schetky. *Library and Archives Canada/W.H. Coverdale collection of Canadiana/C-041888.*

was fatally conspicuous, standing on a carronade-slide, received a ball through his abdomen from the hand of Lieut. Law, of the marines. He fell, severely wounded, and, after four days of suffering, doomed to die.

It was as he lay wounded that Lawrence uttered words that can't exactly be known, but which approximated what would become the slogan of the U.S. Navy: "Don't give up the ship."

The crew of the *Shannon* boarded the *Chesapeake* and fought hand to hand. Broke was injured.

The encounter between the USS Chesapeake and HMS Shannon, diagrammed by time of day and position of sails. The Mariners' Museum, Newport News, Virginia.

Broke parried the pike of his first assailant and wounded him in the face. Before he could recover his guard the second foe struck him with a cutlass on the side of the head; and, instantly on this, the third American, having clubbed the musket, drove home his comrade's weapon, until a large surface of the skull was cloven entirely away—the brain was left bare. Broke sank, of necessity, stunned and bleeding, on the deck; his sword fell from his relaxing grasp, and his first assailant, who had already fallen, strove to muster sufficient strength to consummate the attack. At this moment a marine bayoneted the immediate opponent of the

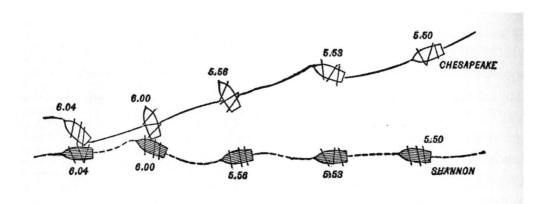

Chesapeake Struck by	*Shannon* Struck .by
29 eighteen-pound shot.	12 eighteen-pound shot.
25 thirty-two pound shot.	13 thirty-two pound shot.
2 nine-pound shot.	14 bar shot.
306 grape.	119 grape.
362 shot.	158 shot.

captain, whilst the enraged Shannons almost literally cut his companions to pieces. It was truly a sanguinary scene. Broke was scarcely to be recognized, even by his own comrades. He was plaistered with lime and blood. Mr. Smith and Mindham, however, tenderly raised him; and, whilst the latter bound an old handkerchief round his captain's streaming head, he applied a

As James Lawrence is mortally wounded, he commands, "Don't Give Up the Ship!" *The Mariners' Museum, Newport News, Virginia.*

It was customary on U.S. Navy ships to find guns painted or engraved with nicknames. Some of the names of *Chesapeake* guns included:

True Blue
Yankee Protection
Putnam
Liberty Forever
Mad Anthony
Liberty or Death
Jumping Billy
Wilful [*sic*] Murder
Pocahontas
Nancy Dawson

The most famous Nancy Dawson of the times was a highly esteemed mid-eighteenth-century dancer with the Covent Garden Playhouse in London. Nancy Dawson died in 1767, and was buried in the Chapel of St. George the Martyr, Queen Square, Bloomsbury. Her tombstone held only the simple epitaph, "Here lies Nancy Dawson." The tune of a song written in her honor became the tune for the children's song "Here We Go 'Round the Mulberry Bush."

What James Lawrence Said

Don't give up the ship!
–commonly accepted

Tell the men to fire faster. Fight 'til she sinks, boys. Don't give up the ship!
–commonly accepted

Tell the men to fire faster, and not give up the ship—the colors shall wave while I live!
–Lieutenant Budd's official account of the action, dated June 15, 1813

Never strike the flag of my ship!
–James Fenimore Cooper's account

Don't give up the boat!
–the *Telegraph*, England

Other variations are given in varying historical accounts of the action. It may be the case that Lawrence uttered variations of the command several different times as he lay wounded on the deck. Also see page 128.

The officers and crew of the *Shannon*, commanded by Captain Broke, board and capture the *Chesapeake*. Published in England, circa 1813. *U.S. Naval Historical Center*.

strong mental cordial by directing his good aft, with the cheering words, "Look there, sir; there goes the old ensign up over the Yankee colours!"

The Result

The battle was now over, and the victory won, according to the most careful and largest computation of the time, in thirteen minutes. In this brief space 252 men were either killed or wounded in the two ships…Fresh reinforcements of Shannons were now sent on board the Chesapeake, conveying back to the English ship her gallant Captain Broke, and the first lieutenant of the enemy (Augustus Ludlow), both severely, and the latter, as it turned out, mortally wounded. Captain Broke was laid in his own cot, in his own cabin, his "good old sword" ("Pray," said he, "take care of my good old sword") being laid beside him. Lieut. Ludlow (who in the hurry of the moment, was left for a little while lying unnoticed in the steerage) sent a touching message—"Will you tell the commanding officer of the Shannon that Mr. Ludlow, first of the Chesapeake, is lying here badly wounded?" He was immediately placed in the berth of poor Watt. And Captain Lawrence, who, on receiving his wound, had been conveyed, in consequence of the shattered state of his cabin, to the Chesapeake's wardroom, remained there—in four days to breathe his last.

Halifax Harbour, circa 1793. Citadel Hill rises up from the waterfront. Its commanding view of the harbour and surrounding territory made it militarily strategic in the North Atlantic, giving Halifax the nickname "Warden of the North." *Library and Archives Canada/W.H. Coverdale collection of Canadiana/C-040112.*

**From "The Chesapeake and Shannon,"
traditional Nova Scotia song**

The *Chesapeake* mounted forty-nine guns
With four hundred and twenty of *Columbia*'s
 picked sons,
The Yankees thought they would never run,
The Yankees thought they would never run.
They being all picked Yankee heroes.

The *Shannon* mounted guns the same
With less men but of better fame,
To beat those Yankees it was their aim,
To beat those Yankees it was their aim
To show them, Rule Britannia.

Up spoke our gallant Captain Broke,
To bet those yanks it is no joke.
Your guns sponge well and make them tell
For Yankees they don't like the smell
Of British balls and powder.

Bold Wallis being next in command
So boldly on the deck did stand,
Saying, "Fire on brave boys, the day's our won
Since Bunker hill brought forth a groan,
The *Chesapeake* is falling."

The HMS *Asia*
and the House of
the Commissioner,
Royal Naval
Dockyards, Halifax,
circa 1797. *Library
and Archives Canada
Peter Winkworth
Collection of
Canadiana.*

Augustus Ludlow of New York, second in command of the USS *Chesapeake*, would die with his captain. And with Broke badly injured, the *Shannon* and her prize headed north toward Nova Scotia, both ships under the command of Provo Wallis.

In 1813, Halifax was the flywheel of the North Atlantic. Its wharves and streets roiled with the accumulated energies of all that had been wrong between the United States and Great Britain since 1776. It had become the North American base of the Royal Navy and its shipyards, accumulator of prizes taken from the United States and France and the easternmost face to the world of all of Canada. Its population of ten thousand ranged from the prime actors of diplomacy, trade and the military to murderers and barefoot prostitutes. Sixteen hundred people worked in the shipyards. Press gangs and thugs roamed the wharves. In a heavy rain, the detritus of the slums at the top of Citadel Hill would flow down past the mansions and government buildings of Barrington Street. Disease was indiscriminate, and smallpox would exact significant reductions in population in the winter of 1814–15.

The *Chesapeake* and *Shannon* enter Halifax Harbour. The painting, attributed to Provo Wallis, corrects the famous Schetky painting of the event (seen on the cover of this book), in which the *Chesapeake* flies a white ensign instead of the blue ensign that Wallis claimed to have raised above the American flag. *The Mariners' Museum, Newport News, Virginia.*

Provo Wallis
With both James
Lawrence and P.B.V.
Broke wounded,
it fell to Wallis to
command both ships
on a dangerous
return to Halifax.
He went on to
become a naval
aide-de-camp to
Queen Victoria,
was knighted in
1860 and made full
admiral in 1863. It
was a custom that
most senior officers
in the Royal Navy
were retained on
active duty lists
for their lifetimes.
But when Wallis
turned ninety-five,
the admiralty urged
his retirement.
Wallis refused
and the admiralty
responded that he
would therefore be
liable for sea duty.
He replied that he
did not know much
about the iron and
steam vessels of
the day, but that he
would be delighted
to see service again.
The matter was
dropped.

But Halifax was, and would remain, a city with a heart. It took in escaped slaves from the American South, found them shelter and clothed them for the winter with old naval uniforms. At the center of the troubled Atlantic community, it offered a harbour for the dispossessed of those troubles. And it was particularly tuned into the human dimensions of the naval war that took place in the ocean that came to its wharves and piers.

Its most prominent church was St. Paul's, the "First Garrison Church" of the military and civilian residents of Halifax, and since 1750 the place where the important events of the larger world first became known. So it was that on Sunday, June 6, 1813, the rector saw his flock suddenly stand up and leave the church mid-sermon. Walking down toward the harbour, the parishioners watched as the *Shannon*, captained by their own Provo Wallis, brought her prize, the *Chesapeake*, up to the King's Wharf. After months at sea and battle, the *Shannon* looked dirty and run-down, but, having just been refurbished and despite her battle scars, the *Chesapeake* was freshly painted and sparkling in the sun. Her true condition, however, would later be entered into the annals of Nova Scotian literature.

The Clockmaker; or the Sayings and Doings of Samuel Slick of Slickville by Thomas Chandler Haliburton was the first in a series of satirical sketches of Nova Scotian life published in the Halifax newspaper the *Nova Scotian* in 1835, and later published internationally in book form. Haliburton was a lawyer and judge who would eventually become a member of the British Parliament. Though written more than twenty years after the fact, the story of the *Chesapeake* was still important enough in Nova Scotian lore to be included in *The Clockmaker*, though in a decidedly sober way. Samuel Slick/Thomas Haliburton had managed to sneak onto the ship not long after it arrived in Halifax. It was a scene, he wrote,

> *never to be forgotten by a landsman. The deck had not been cleaned…and the coils and folds of rope were steeped in gore as if in a slaughter-house. She was a fir built ship and her splinters had wounded as many men as the Shannon's shot. Pieces of skin, with pendant hair, were adhering to the sides of the ship; and in one place I noticed pieces of fingers protruding…Altogether it was a scene as difficult to forget as to describe. It is one of the most painful reminiscences of my youth.*

Nor did the Haligonians make light of the arrival of the *Chesapeake* in their harbour. As word got around to the rest of the city's churches, the people crowded the wharves and shoreline. On her main deck, as she grew closer, everyone could see the large body of her captain, James Lawrence, shrouded in the American flag.

There was great pride that the two ships had been brought into the harbour by Provo Wallis, one of their own, but there were no reports of cheering in the streets of Halifax. In a day when naval commanders were widely known and storied on both sides of a war, Lawrence was revered as a man of compassion and good heart who had treated his British prisoners well when he took them, particularly in the battle of the *Hornet* and the *Peacock*. His body would be treated with the highest of honors by the British and Nova Scotians. The garrison issued its orders:

> *7th June 1813.*
>
> *A funeral party will be furnished to-morrow, by the 64th regiment, consisting of 300 rank and file, with a proper proportion of officers, and to be supplied with three rounds of blank cartridge each man, to inter the remains of Captain Lawrence, late of the American frigate Chesapeake, from the King's Wharf, at half-past one o'clock p.m. The band of that corps will attend, and the party will be commanded by Lieutenant-Colonel Sir J. Wardlaw. The officers of the garrison will be pleased to attend the commandant there, at a quarter before two, to march in procession, wearing a piece of black crape around the left arm.*
>
> *(Signed) F.T. THOMAS,*
> *Major of Brigade*

Portion of a drawing in the magazine *Punch*, volume 100, dated April 25, 1891, and captioned: "The Senior Admiral of the Fleet, SIR PROVO WILLIAM PARRY WALLIS, G.C.B., who was in the action between the British Frigate *Shannon* and the American Frigate *Chesapeake* on June 1st, 1813 (taking command of the *Shannon* after the disabling of Captain BROKE), celebrated the hundredth anniversary of his birthday on April 12th, 1891."

Lawrence's mahogany coffin was one of three taken from the *Chesapeake* that day. They were placed on a twelve-oared barge and rowed in short strokes to King's Wharf. A witness, quoted in the biography of P.B.V. Broke, wrote,

> *The procession was very long, and everything was conducted in the most solemn and respectful manner; and the wounded officers of both nations, who followed in the procession, made the scene very effecting. I never attended a funeral in my life where my feelings were so much struck. There was not the least mark of exultation, that I saw, even among the commonest people. All appeared to lament his death; and I heard several say they considered the blood shed on the Chesapeake's deck as dear as that of their own countrymen.*

Also buried at the Old Burying Grounds is British Major General Robert Ross. In the War of 1812, he was in charge of all British forces on the East Coast, and led the Battle of Bladensburg (Maryland) in defeat of American forces. Moving on to Washington, he is credited with commanding or inspiring the destruction of the Capitol and the White House. His end came with defeat in the Battle of Baltimore, inspiring Francis Scott Key to write the "Star-Spangled Banner." His body was preserved in a 129-gallon barrel of Jamaican rum for transport to Halifax. *Courtesy of the author.*

James Lawrence was buried in St. Paul's Old Burying Grounds on Barrington Street. James Fenimore Cooper would summarize his life: "There was no more dodge in him than there was in the mainmast."

Some of the *Chesapeake* sailors were marched over Citadel Hill to the prison at Melville Island. Some of the dead were buried in the graveyard at Deadman's Island.

A summary of events under P.B.V. Broke's name would report to his superiors, "The Chesapeake is a fine frigate, and mounts forty-nine guns, eighteen-pounders on her main deck, thirty-two-pounders on her quarterdeck and forecastle. Both ships came out of action in the most beautiful order, their rigging appearing as perfect as if they had only been exchanging a salute."

And the prize, *Chesapeake*, was taken east into the Atlantic toward England.

GLORIOUS VICTORY,
CAPTAIN BROKE, OF THE SHANNON,
38 guns & 270 brave men,
Has Challenged, Fought, and in Fifteen Minutes took the INSOLENT CHESAPEAKE, (Principal Cause of the American War,) mounting 50 Guns and 400 Men.

Courtesy of southernlife.org.uk.

Chapter 4

The Plowshare

The Meon River begins as a spring in the South Downs of southern England. It gains strength from surface and ground waters as it first heads northwest to East Meon and Drayton, and then turns south at West Meon. Along the way it flows in and out of irrigation channels, and enters the top of Wickham Parish, County of Hampshire, ninety feet above sea level. It accelerates through the town, leaving the bottom of the parish at twenty-five feet above sea level before reaching the Solent, another six miles distant. Throughout its history it has powered fifteen known water mills, large and small, and most naturally the mills at Wickham, where its force was perhaps the strongest.

The first wooden bridge across the Meon was probably built in Roman times just south of Wickham as part of an infrastructure development by the Romans that would put the town permanently at a crossroads of trade and history, and on the well-traveled road between Winchester and Chichester. It wasn't until 826, however, that the town, then more of a manor, appeared in official documents as a boundary of a land grant from King Egbert.

In 1086, King William I, William the Conqueror, oversaw, for taxation purposes, an inventory of all of the lands and resources in his domain. The assay took about a year, and eventually noted every tool, animal, plot of land and building that could be found and assessed, included in a two-volume, handwritten document. "There was no single hide nor a yard of land, nor indeed one ox nor one cow nor one pig which was left out," noted one observer. Thus it came to be called the *Domesday Book*, after the Doomsday described in the Bible as the time of last judgment. What went into the *Domesday Book* could not be deleted, and it would stand in judgment for all eternity. In modern times, it is one of the most astounding of historical documents, and in its own time it was a new milestone in the accumulation of British history.

The *Domesday Book* gives the first real information about Wickham: that it consisted of, among other things, two manors, land for seven

Wickham

First "wichaema," AD 826. Probably from the Roman form "vicus" and meaning "small Roman town or villa complex."

Meon River

Believed related in name to the river Main in Germany.

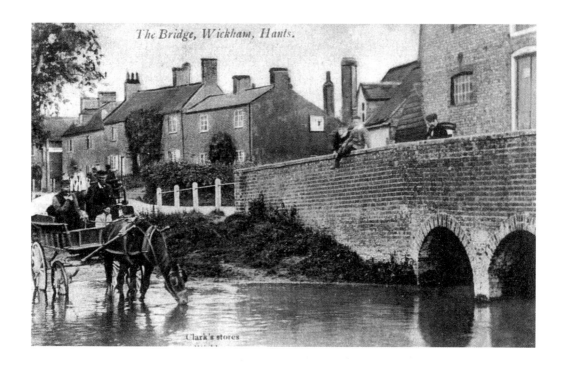

The Bridge, Wickham, Hants.

Clark's stores

The Meon River near the Fareham Road Bridge, late 1880s. Wickham History Society.

ploughs, an eight-acre meadow, five slaves in the labor force and two mills, for a total value of £7. Twenty-two shillings of that value were attributed to the mills, which were not fully constructed water mills, but the millstones that they used which could be more valuable than the structures in which they worked.

In the industrial archaeology of Great Britain, its first water mills are lost in the mists of time. But most every village that had a river or stream had a mill for some portion of its history. Beginning in the late Middle Ages, coastal communities, or those on tidal waters, developed tidal mills. Powered by the moon, they were the most reliable motive power available. "A river might dry up," said Tony Yoward of modern-day Britain's Hampshire Mills Group, "wind might not blow, but the good Lord sent the tide in twice a day. In an age of uncertainty you were absolutely certain you could mill." The mills of Britain were the workhorses of the centuries; more than two hundred of them can be identified in the history of the County of Hampshire. Nationwide, they performed more than a hundred manufacturing processes, ranging from the production of ciders and dyes to iron and cloth. In the vicinity of Portsmouth, the remnants of ten water mills, four tidal mills and three windmills could still be found in the late twentieth century. Through the centuries, the Meon River was the life force of Wickham, and

Wickham Fair on the village square, early 1900s. *Wickham History Society.*

not just as a driver of its mills. It filled the water meadows that controlled flooding and produced the first sources of spring hay and cattle feed. Fresh water came from its tributaries, along with industrial water for manufacturing, cleaning and disposal. It was used by animals for nourishment and as a depository of waste.

In 1269, King Henry III granted a charter to Lord of the Manor Roger de Scures "that he an his heirs may have free warren in all the demesne lands of his manor of Wykham in the [then] county of Southampton forever." The charter denoted Wickham, bisected by the Meon, as a market town, a designation that protected the trade of one region from being encroached upon by another. The size of the region was generally determined by distances that would allow a trader to walk to the market, sell his goods and return home in one day. An annual Wickham Fair was set for May 9 of each year; after the adoption of the Gregorian calendar, this date was changed to May 20, and continues on that date into the twenty-first century.

It was about that time that the town and its large square were permanently fixed into its current location. And, according to Barrie Marson of the Wickham History Society, the town as seen now is pretty much as it was seen then: a planned community, laid out in the form of burgage plots—pieces of land just big enough to feed and house a single family—which still delineate the modern town.

Wickham's development as a market and milling town was accelerated in the Tudor era through the seventeenth century. Farmers and manufacturers became merchants, and, situated between the larger towns of Winchester and Chichester, the cities and ports of Southampton and Portsmouth just to the south, there was more than enough business to go around. The Royal Dockyards of Portsmouth were large consumers of timbers felled in the nearby Forest of Bere, carpentered in the town and taken away by oxen cartage. The foodstuffs and clothing needs of the navy were supplied by the mills, tailors and farmers of the County of Hampshire, and as the next centuries of British naval expansion and conflict unfolded, it is no doubt that the mill at Wickham supplied the flour and biscuits that went to sea. By the mid-1700s the water meadows fed by the Meon produced an average of two tons of grain per acre, much of it to be taken to the mill, and a percentage of it to be given to the miller in exchange for his work.

As the Napoleonic Wars of the late 1700s pressed down upon Britain, the roads and bridges of the County of Hampshire were necessarily improved by acts of Parliament. On high land just east of the village, a telegraph station was constructed as part of a string of such stations that extended, tightly spaced, over the eighty miles from London to the dockyards of the Solent. Weather permitting, a signaled message could be sent from pole to pole along the entire length of the system within minutes. And Wickham was also a smugglers' town. Goods from elsewhere on the English Channel were brought to the unguarded shores of the Solent, and were taken up the Meon to be hidden there before distribution farther inland.

It was in the midst of this prosperity that Thomas Prior purchased the mill at Wickham in 1784. It had three pairs of millstones, and spanned the river, including cottages and a garden on its grounds. In 1819, Prior's son John decided to tear it down and construct a new and more modern mill in its place.

As the defeated American frigate, the unlucky ship, headed east out of Halifax in June of 1813, she forever ceased to be the USS *Chesapeake* and would soon become the HMS *Chesapeake*. News of her defeat had been sped to London on the British ship *Nova Scotia*, and it was met with great acclaim. The British had been chastened by the relative sluggishness of their navy during the war, and their success at this one confrontation was used to overcome their chagrin at previous failures. The *Chesapeake* was indeed a prize. The British found the U.S. Navy signal books in her precincts. The codes were in the hands of British captains heading out of Portsmouth within six weeks, but the U.S. Navy moved quickly to limit the damage by changing its signals in ways that would give the advantage to the Americans if the British used the captured codes.

The *London Gazette*
of July 6–10,
1813, published
an account of the
battle attributed to
Provo Wallis, though
probably written by
a subordinate: "The
enemy came down
in a very handsome
manner, having
three American
ensigns flying; when
closing with us
he sent down his
royal yards. I kept
the *Shannon*'s up,
expecting the breeze
would die away. At
half past five P.M.
the enemy hauled
up within hail of
us on the starboard
side, and the battle
began, both ships
steering full under
the topsails."

The *Chesapeake* was, too, the first of the six frigates taken prize
by the British (the USS *President* would be surrendered by Stephen
Decatur off Long Island on January 15, 1815), and would be the
subject of study by the British as they sent her back into the war
under her new flag. Thus, the Virginia Calendar of State papers
held this entry of April 13, 1814, by John G. Joynes (adjutant,
Second Virginia Regiment), posted from Onancock on Virginia's
Eastern Shore:

> *In obedience to your orders of yesterday requiring me to make you
> a correct statement of the Enemy's force, I make you the following
> report which I have collected from the different posts on duty and
> from Thomas Sharrod, who has been on board the Admiral's
> Ship. There are 6 ships in view: the Albion, 74, Admiral*

Cockburn; 1 the Chesapeake, late U.S. frigate; the 50 Gun Ship Armede, Trowbridge; the others all appear to be frigates…We have on duty about 200 men, which is too small a force to defend our extensive Bay Coast exposed to the enemy. Upon an examination of Thos. Sharrod, he says that the enemy said they intended, as soon as they could make proper arrangements on the Island [they had occupied Tangier Island], *to send a flag on shore demanding of us provisions, and in case it was refused, they intended to land a sufficient force to take such supplies as they wanted, and they would scour the whole country.*

The Troops on duty are in high spirits, and had much rather risque an engagement than be so frequently harassed.

History does not record that the HMS *Chesapeake* was forced to follow through on an attack against the settlements of her namesake bay, but the casual mention of the ship as "late U.S. frigate" seemed to be in keeping with both an American attitude about its former unlucky frigate and the fact of life of naval ships of the time, in that they passed back and forth between enemies on occasion. Another part of that philosophy about the destiny of sailing ships, particularly as it was held by the British, would contribute to the *Chesapeake*'s fortunes in the following centuries. It was that they were ultimately recyclable, especially in the island nation of Great Britain. So it was that after her sighting in the Chesapeake Bay, the *Chesapeake* worked convoys between England and the Cape of Good Hope for a time; with no sense of irony carried prisoners from Melville Island in Halifax to Dartmoor Prison in England; fell into use either as a stores ship or prison hulk in Portsmouth Harbour; and showed up again in a newspaper ad in the *Hampshire Telegraph and Sussex Chronicle* of April 17, 1820. The ad was read by the miller John Prior, or one of his agents.

> SUPERIOR SHIP TIMBER.
> To Gentlemen, Farmers, Ship and House Buil-
> ders, Smiths, and Others:
> THE HULLS of his Majesty's late Ships,
> CHESAPEAKE and CHERUB, are now breaking up
> at Pesthouse, near Portsea, where there is for Sale, a
> very large quantity of OAK and FIR TIMBER, of
> most excellent quality, and well worth the attention of
> any person; consisting of 150 Oak and Fir Beams, of
> the following sizes—5 by 7, 7 by 9, 8 by 10, 12 by 15,
> from 20 to 40 feet long; Oak and Fir Plank 2½, 3, 4, 5,
> 6, and 7 inches of long lengths, from 40 to 70 feet,
> Floors, Futticks, Top Timbers, Knees, Carlins,
> Ledges, Cabin Fittings, and a larger and more supe-
> rior assortment of Ship Timber, than was ever before
> offered to the Public.
> Also, an excellent double Capstan, about 30 Tons of
> Swedish Iron, Spikes, Bolts, and about 30 Iron Knees.
> The above may be Shipped free of expence, being
> close to the water.—For particulars, enquire of Jo-
> seph Pushman and Co. on the Premises.

By 1820, Great Britain had an exceedingly excessive inventory of wooden naval ships. The War of 1812 had come to a vague conclusion with the signing of the Treaty of Ghent in December 1814. It was vague because, started in a miscommunication, the war seemed to many to have had no purpose, resulted in no changes of borders and ended without an exclamation point. The matter of impressments was no longer a problem, and wasn't mentioned in the treaty.

In the fullness of history, however, the war gave definition to the centuries that would follow. Canadian North America, having resisted U.S. advances on its territory, had a strengthened sense of itself and a new measure of unity between French- and English-speaking Canadians. They would gain a healthy distrust of their southern neighbor, and eventually their own independence from the British in 1867. Canadian historian Arthur Lower wrote, "It therefore does not seem too far out to say that the War of 1812 is one of the massive foundation stones of modern Canada." Native tribes, however, hopeful that events would return lost land and autonomy, saw those hopes dashed. America and England recovered to emerge as enduring friends and allies. A century later, the war was virtually forgotten.

If it had not been for you English I should have been emperor of the East, but wherever there is water to float a ship we are sure to find you in our way.
–Napoleon Bonaparte as he surrendered on the HMS *Bellerophon*, July 15, 1815

When the Battle of Waterloo brought a conclusion in Britain's favor to the Napoleonic Wars in June 1815, the wind was turned to a gentle breeze against the sails of the Royal Navy. All of that wood, acquired from all over the world through harvesting or prize-taking, could now be recycled into other purposes. It formed new piers and jetties, or was saved for future construction. Much of it went into the postwar building of homes and businesses. Oak that had traveled the seas became tables and desks. Damaged wood became firewood. The thickest and longest of beams became parts of churches and farm buildings. But the only large portion of one ship's wood that would be traced into the twenty-first century would be the portion of the *Chesapeake* purchased by John Prior, taken by water to Fareham and carted overland to the mill site in Wickham.

George Brighton's biography of P.B.V. Broke contains a letter from the vicar of Fareham, dated April 9, 1864, excerpted here:

> *Mr. Prior pulled down his own mill at Wickham, and constructed a new one with this timber, which he found admirably adapted for the purpose. The deck timbers were thirty-two feet long and eighteen inches square, and were placed, unaltered, horizontally in the mill. The purlins of the deck were about twelve feet long, and served, without alteration, for joists. The mill, still in existence and in active operation (the property of Mr. Goderick) stands just as Mr. Prior erected it in 1820, and is likely to last yet hundreds of years. Mr. Prior is now living in Farnham, and I have just taken the foregoing information from his lips.*

I remain, dear Sir,
Very faithfully yours,

W.S. Dumergue

What is most important in the vicar's reporting is that the timbers, purlins and other wood not mentioned were used in the new mill as they were taken from the ship. Thus, the ship gave shape and dimension to the mill. Then the ship's wood was given the protection of brick walls and a roof that would make it "likely to last yet hundreds of years." The building erected in 1820 remained barely changed in the first two of those hundreds of years.

County of Hampshire and Wickham historian Bruce Tappenden was the last of the millers to own the structure in the late twentieth century. He wrote an extensive dissertation on its history while studying at the University of Portsmouth, and described

> *a substantial rectangular building in brick, of three stories with a tiled, half mansared roof…built on very deep and substantial brick foundation that goes down into the gravel of the old river bed…the beams and trusses to the roof are less substantial than the beams lower down the mill, only having to support the roof and are therefore not load bearing…in former days it was quite common practice in mills not to carry the floor boarding to the walls but to leave a space around the walls. This served two useful functions, it improved ventilation and also facilitated the emptying of sacks into the storage bins on the floor below.*

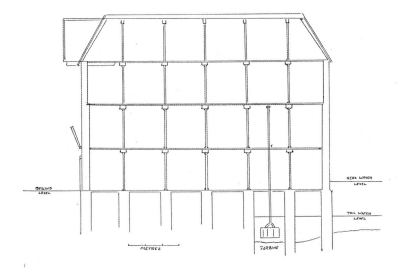

A simple schematic of Chesapeake Mill. *From* The Mill at Wickham, Hampshire—*J.B. Tappenden, 1986.*

At its construction in 1820 it was named the Chesapeake Mill, and was considered to be very modern in design. Its power was derived from two breast-shot water wheels (situated to turn in the opposite direction of the water flow) to drive five pair of millstones and assorted hauling mechanisms. It used cast-iron rather than wooden gearing, and a drying kiln to prepare the grain for easier milling. It employed up to ten people at times of peak production. At the river it used a bypass sluice for the heavy rains of winter, and a fish router to allow salmon to go to sea.

But if the mill was likely to last hundreds of years, its function was not. In retrospect, the considerable investment in its rebuilding with the strong American pine taken from the *Chesapeake* may have been badly timed. Just as the end of the wars had left a surplus of wooden navy ships, including the *Chesapeake*, it had also left a surplus of milling capacity in the County of Hampshire. The mill would be sold out of the Prior family in 1826, the first of many changes in ownership over the next 150 years. It was not until 1864 that the mill came to the attention of the Reverend George Brighton, occasioning the letter returned to him from the vicar of Fareham.

"The receipt of this letter," he wrote, "set me again on historical pilgrimage. The longing was irresistible to see for oneself this strange metamorphose of a sanguinary man-of-war into a peaceful, life-sustaining cornmill. I had pictured it all to myself, most exactly;

A layshaft on the first floor of Chesapeake Mill received the main belt drive from the water turbine, thereby turning the shaft to its left (pictured with belt still attached), transmitting the drive to upper floors. *Hampshire Mills Group.*

but, like all other imaginary realizations of persons and places, nothing could be more dissimilar than the reality."

On a wet July day, Brighton traveled by train from London's Waterloo station to Fareham.

At this latter place a change of vehicle conveyed me, more slowly, through an undulating, picturesque, and well-wooded district. Bye and bye a valley opened, through which a stream might be conjectured to flow; and after a few turns more the "fly," with a grating check, drew up before a comely house of three stories and a range of dormer windows in the roof. Nothing shiplike or of the sea was discernible from without.

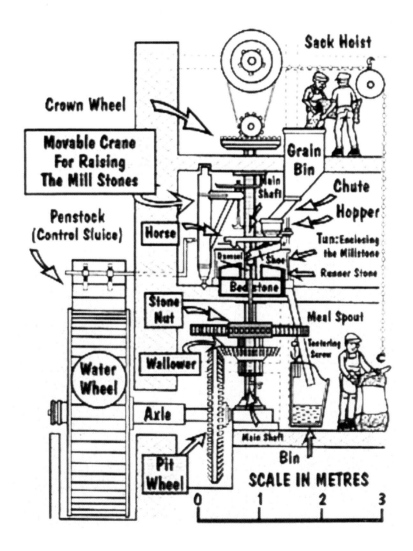

Operating mechanism of a typical water mill. *Hampshire Mills Group.*

But, once inside, the biographer of P.B.V. Broke found himself transported back to what seemed to him to have been an exquisite moment in a ship at sea. "On every floor," he wrote, "the blithe and mealy men were urging their life-sustaining toil. But, my reader, on one of those planks, on one of these floors, beyond all reasonable doubt, Lawrence fell, in the writhing anguish of his mortal wound…and on others Broke lay ensanguined, and his assailants dead, while nearby Ludlow must have poured out his life's blood."

He continued, perhaps offering the first turn of a phrase that would be uttered by like-minded people in future centuries.

Perhaps, thought I, at last, it is better this should be the end of the proud Chesapeake. The dream of glory (and never was one more lofty) lives and long shall live upon the page of history; but one day of this tranquil toil in God's holy name and love would, I think, be infinitely more valued by Philip Broke now than would the capture of a thousand Chesapeakes; for he is hard on the confines of that glorious land, where in the sublime language of the sacred prophet "Shall go no galley without oars, neither shall gallant ship pass thereby; and where nations shall make war no more."

This last phrase appears to be the reverend's personal addition to Isaiah 33:21.

Some years later, author Edgar Stanton MacLay, in *A History of the United States Navy, from 1775 to 1893*, would refer to Brighton in offering his own biblical conclusion that "the metamorphosis of a sanguinary man-of-war into a peaceful flour mill is perhaps as near an approach to the Scriptural prophecy that spears and swords

Right: "The blithe and mealy men were urging their life-sustaining toil." An interior drawing of the mill, circa 1864. *From* Admiral P.B.V. Broke—A Memoir *by George Brighton.*

Left: A postcard depicting the mill as "a place of pilgrimage for all Americans," circa 1910. *Wickham History Society.*

Great Fontley Farm and its farmhouse date to the early sixteenth century. It was likely a provider of grain to the Chesapeake Mill. Its twentieth-century owners were livestock farmers, and purchased feed from the mill until it closed. *Wickham History Society.*

shall be beaten into plows and pruning-hooks as the conditions of modern civilization will allow."

By the year following Brighton's visit, the Chesapeake Mill had gained a steam engine to supplement its water power, and installed mills and rollers of more efficient design. In 1865, operation of the mill was taken over by a twenty-one-year lease. An extraordinary inventory accompanying the leasehold listed everything from finger plates on the walls, to large and small machinery, furniture and even various sizes of "Swiss Dressing Cloths." Historian and mill owner Bruce Tappenden noted in his dissertation of 1986 that the document held the potential of a great contribution to industrial archaeology.

The last half of the nineteenth century would mark the beginning of change and decline in British milling. The smaller village mills scattered about had already begun closing, their work migrating to larger mills like the one at Wickham. Then the development of steam technologies and the way trade moved across the oceans of the world began to move milling to the ports and larger cities. And there was the matter of what kind of bread people wanted to eat.

Whole wheat and rye breads had long been the staple of the British commoner, but white bread was considered a luxury for the upper classes. And bread was a cause of social conflict in the early nineteenth century. The Corn Laws of 1815 had been passed to protect the markets of British wheat growers by increasing the tariffs on imported grain, but by mid-century, bread had become too expensive, leading to social unrest. The Corn Laws were repealed, and the progress of international shipping matched the repeal with the import of grain from the prairies of Canada, the

An early photograph of the mill under ownership of the Edney family. *The Chesapeake Mill.*

United States and Australia. The foreign grain was not only less expensive, but it was also better suited to the production of white bread, and that, in turn, was enhanced by the development of new milling technologies that began to be located at the ports. Thus it was that foreign wheat was milled at the ports of Southampton and Liverpool, among others, by roller mills driven by steam engines. They took market share from water mills in smaller towns like Wickham. Railroads allowed the movement of port-milled wheat farther into the countryside.

Between 1855 and 1919, the Chesapeake Mill was churned through seven owners. Steam turbines, imported from America, came on line in the late 1800s. The mill's own use of coal-fired steam power matched the increasing use of steam by local farmers, and put it in the business of coal sales for a number of years. But the path was set. Bruce Tappenden noted that by the end of the nineteenth century "it was in a derelict state, with its proprietor bankrupt...In this village the mill, or at any rate the site of the mill, is even older than the Parish Church. It had ground corn since time immemorial and would continue to serve future generations, but for a number of reasons this established order had come to an end by the close of the century."

At the turn of the new century, the commerce of Wickham began to decline further. The once much-needed tannery had become unnecessary a few decades earlier. The town brewery, across Bridge Street from the mill, was put out of business by national brewers

This photograph of the mill's interior, showing both its maritime and agricultural qualities, circa 1930s, is the picture of the mill most known to naval historians. *The Mariners' Museum, Newport News, Virginia.*

in 1911. In 1913, the mill was acquired by the Edney family, and a new effort at modernization of milling and marketing was undertaken. The mill traded more heavily on its namesake frigate, placed a silhouette of the ship on its grain bags and promoted itself as "a place of pilgrimage for all Americans," which was not exactly true. Town legends in Wickham recounted the sounds of ghosts and battles emitting from the building late at night.

As the years progressed, the mill ceased to produce flour and moved into the non-milling production of cattle feeds, and finally to food for dogs and cats. Bruce Tappenden was a member of the Edney family by marriage. In 1986, he gave it one last bit of glory with the following invitation to friends, interested parties and the U.S. ambassador to Britain:

> *You are hereby invited to attend celebration to commemorate the One hundred and Seventy Third anniversary of the taking in battle of the American frigate "Chesapeake" by His Britannic Majesty King George the Third's ship "Shannon" on the first day of June in the Fifty Third year of his reign anno domini One Thousand Eight Hundred and Thirteen.*

Metal placards advertising Spratts and Melox dog foods within the mill. *The Chesapeake Mill.*

The aforementioned celebration to be held in those premises now known as—The Chesapeake Mill—situate in the Parish of Wickham and now in the tenure of Sylvia and Bruce Tappenden of the said Parish. Commencing at twelve noon. The herein-referred to-above mentioned event will take place on the First day of June in the year One Thousand Nine Hundred and Eighty Six. Long live the Queen.

Bruce Tappenden beneath the timbers of the USS *Chesapeake*, December 30, 1996. The headline predicts a "US tourist Bonanza" that has not taken place. *The* News, *Portsmouth, www. portsmouth.co.uk.*

The News, Monday, December 30, 1996

WICKHAM | *Landmark mill contains timbers from famous warship*

Chip off historic block may herald US tourist bonanza

■ *Discovery adds impetus to major plans for restoration.*

By NEIL DURHAM
The News

Wickham could grab a slice of the American tourism trade thanks to a disused mill at the heart of new heritage centre.

An expert has confirmed that Chesapeake Mill contains timbers from the celebrated U.S. wooden warship of the same name.

Locals have long believed the mill's connections with the USS Chesapeake, which was captured by the British in Boston Bay in 1813.

But now it has been confirmed after a visit by Brian Lavery, curator of ship technology at the National Maritime Museum in Greenwich, south London.

The find adds weight to a group's campaign for National Lottery funding to

USS Chesapeake

Historian Bruce Tappenden surveys beams at Wickham Mill which came from the USS Chesapeake

The English mill built of the timbers of an unlucky American frigate was closed two years later. It sat empty on Bridge Street. Barrie Marson of the Wickham History Society remembered that "it was all a bit sad in its dying days. It had lots of visitors who wanted to have a look, half because of the *Chesapeake* and half because of the milling. There was a hope that someone would preserve it as a working mill." But that was not to be. It became, said Marson, "almost an eyesore, many of its windows broken, pigeons flying in and out, using it as a home."

CHAPTER 5

THE RETURN

Oh, better that her shattered hulk
Should sink beneath the wave;
Her thunders shook the mighty deep,
And there should be her grave;
Nail to the mast her holy flag,
Set every threadbare sail,
And give her to the god of storms,
The lightning and the gale!
—"Old Ironsides," Oliver Wendel Holmes Sr., 1830

If the War of 1812 had brought the United States to the next
step of knowledge of its sovereignty and potential, an 1830
incident involving the USS *Constitution* helped to remind the
country that it now had a history. And with history came the
notion of historic preservation. When an article in Boston's *Daily
Advertiser* suggested erroneously that the navy planned to break up
the *Constitution*, an immediate uproar was heard in the land. The
poem by Oliver Wendell Holmes protesting that the ship would
be given more dignity in sinking than in breaking up became the
rallying cry of a movement. Judged un-seaworthy in 1830, she
was reconstructed in 1835 under an act of Congress, the first of a
number of rejuvenations sustaining her into twenty-first-century
life in Boston Harbor.

By that year, the known remains of the USS *Chesapeake* had
already spent fifteen years under the protection of the walls and
roof of an English water mill. They, too, would eventually provoke
the concept of historic preservation, though in a way more complex
than was applied to her sister ship, the *Constitution*.

In 1944, during World War II, Eric Walker was thirteen years
old, one of a multitude of small boys both in awe and in fear of
the war that came raining down from the sky over the County of
Hampshire.

My stepfather, who was in the R.A., was stationed in Wallington Barracks at the top of the hill. The Canadian Tank Regiment had their tanks in the front gardens opposite St Peter & Paul Church. We cadged gum and cigarettes off the yanky servicemen and yes, we smoked behind the bike sheds amongst other things. In early 1944 I lived on Portsdown Hill and it was the "doodlebug" run. You were OK so long as you could see and hear them coming but when the eerie silence was followed by a loud explosion you knew you were OK and that some other poor sod had copped their lot. These were then followed by an even more terrible weapon, the V2. One minute a road with over 100 houses was there, the next large areas of flat surfaces with a lot of smoke.

The USS *Constitution* has always been the symbol of the history and might of the U.S. Navy. It is seen here in a festive celebration of George Washington's birthday in the harbor at Valetta Malta, 1837. *The Mariners' Museum, Newport News, Virginia.*

Eric's stepfather was in charge of prisoners of war held in Hampshire, and would take groups of them to be laborers on the surrounding farms and in the mills, as Eric tagged along. One day they ended up at the mill in Wickham. "There were several American army and navy personnel walking around the mill. And I asked them, you know, 'why are you here? What are you looking for?' And they said 'Well all of this wood came from one of our ships.'" Eric was very interested in wood at that point in his life,

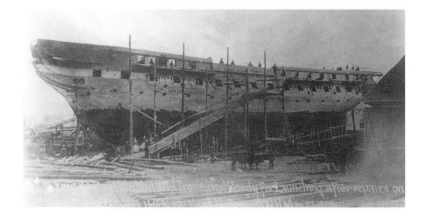

The USS *Constitution* ready for launching after repairs at the U.S. Navy yard at Portsmouth, New Hampshire, May 27, 1858. It was then converted to a navy school ship. *The Mariners' Museum, Newport News, Virginia.*

The restored gun deck of the USS *Constitution*, seen in a visit to Norfolk, Virginia, October 1931. *The Mariners' Museum, Newport News, Virginia.*

and at that moment his lifelong interest in the mill was begun. "I was a very curious little boy," he said. It stayed with him as "my mother delivered me to" the training ship *Arethusa* (née *Peking*) at age fourteen, followed by fifteen years in the Royal Navy and work in the shipwright's department of the historic HMS *Warrior* until his retirement. Over that time, he studied British and American naval history, and became a restorer and sculptor of historic ship figureheads.

At the time of his discovery of the mill, Portsmouth and the dockyards were being relentlessly bombed by the Germans. A reporter for a local newspaper wrote,

I watched German planes crash in flames, their pilots leaping for their lives by parachute when they were trapped in a web of murderous fire during an attack by fifty Nazi aircraft on this vital British naval base. Fires broke out in many parts of Portsmouth, whole rows of houses were wrecked and streets were peppered with shrapnel bits. A civilian hospital caught fire, but the flames were quickly extinguished by asbestos-garbed crews of ARP workers.

Only one attempted firebombing of Wickham is recorded, but it was not successful, and it was the small boys of the town who picked up the shrapnel and rode their bikes into the country to see the sights of crashed German airplanes. Because it was sufficiently inland, Wickham became a refuge for citizens of London, Portsmouth and other coastal towns when housing was destroyed or bombing was

Widespread damage came to Portsmouth, England, in the German air raid of August 12, 1940. Smoke rises above the harbour railroad station. Masts of the HMS *Victory* can be seen at the left. *The* News, *Portsmouth, www.portsmouth.co.uk.*

A bomb in May 1944 left rubble on Newcomen Road and killed fifteen residents. It is probable that the construction and furniture byproducts of many old wooden ships, including those of the USS *Chesapeake*, were destroyed in the war, though many may have been recycled. *The* News, *Portsmouth, www.portsmouth.co.uk.*

too dangerous. Many of its permanent residents were serving in the war and at sea, and every bit of news held the potential for pain. Several units of the Canadian army were in residence around the town, their tanks sometimes hidden in the brush. The war effort was supported by a maternity unit for naval wives in the hospital and a mobile laundry for the troops placed behind the Chesapeake Mill. Women made camouflage nets in the bus garage. Much of the energy of the Meon River Valley in early 1944 was directed toward the coming Allied invasion across the English Channel of the Normandy beaches.

Below the Portsdown Hills, just five miles from Wickham, sat Southwick House, first used as a refuge for the Royal Naval School of Navigation when dockyard bombing increased in 1941. In

Sharing her birthplace with the USS *Chesapeake*, the USS *Herndon* was one of many ships launched from the navy shipyard at Portsmouth, Virginia, in World War II, going down the ways February 2, 1944. Like the *Chesapeake*, she saw service at Algiers and then sailed in the Normandy invasion of June 6, 1944, bombarding enemy emplacements on Omaha Beach. After accompanying Franklin Delano Roosevelt to the Yalta Convention near the end of the European war, she moved on to China and received a vice admiral of the Japanese navy as he surrendered all Japanese vessels in the region of Tsingtao. *Kirn Library, Norfolk, Sargeant Memorial Room.*

The USS *Augusta* was a product of the Newport News Shipbuilding and Drydock Company and the Norfolk Navy Shipyard at Portsmouth, commissioned by the navy in January 1931. In World War II, she hosted the first face to face meeting between President Franklin Delano Roosevelt and Prime Minister Winston Churchill, fought off the shores of Morocco and is seen here participating in the Normandy invasion. Left to right on her bridge are Commander Rear Admiral Alan G. Kirk, USN; General Omar Bradley, commanding general of American ground forces; and Rear Admiral A.D. Strouble. The photo's caption reads, "All keep their eyes concentrated on the Normandy Coast, watching the progress of the battles for France."

The Mariners' Museum, Newport News, Virginia.

1943, the house became forward headquarters of the Supreme Headquarters Allies Expeditionary Force (SHAEF). Its main drawing room became the planning site and map room for the D-Day Invasion, and the virtual home of American General Dwight D. Eisenhower and British General Bernard Montgomery.

On June 6, 1944, an invasion force of nearly 7,000 American, British and Canadian ships, with 195,000 soldiers, marines and sailors of the three nations, set out across the English Channel toward France. A number of the ships had been built or repaired in the former Gosport Shipyard in Portsmouth, Virginia, and in the success of the day's effort, the relationship between the two Portsmouths had been brought full circle. Once parent and child, then enemies, the two cities on opposite sides of the Atlantic were now absolute allies. The twists and turns of their common histories would not be brought to light again until the derelict mill in the County of Hampshire found itself sailing into the treacherous crosswinds of the 1990s.

The mill had sat mostly empty up until 1998, and was last used in that year for storage of animal foods. As various groups and interests had tried to find a new and viable purpose for the building, it fell into further disrepair, and was finally purchased by the County of Hampshire Council, in part to get control of the blight it brought upon the town. There was only the slimmest danger that it could be torn down. It was already listed by English Heritage,

The women
and children of
Wickham gather for
V-E Day in Market
Square. *Wickham
History Society*.

Britain's statutory adviser on the historic environment, as a Grade
II building "of special interest, warranting every effort to preserve."
That protection, however, would not necessarily protect its timbers
from being disfigured in some way. The county's purchase started
the debate about the next chapter in the lives of those timbers, in
earnest.

In the case of the USS *Constitution*, there was little ambiguity.
The twenty-first-century ship in Boston Harbor was an artifact
of American history, though by now it was made up of only 15
to 20 percent of the original ship launched in 1797, and perhaps
much less. But what was the Chesapeake Mill on Bridge Street,
Wickham? The answer to that question became very important to a
lot of people; as important, perhaps, as the answer to the question:
what is history? And it was then that the USS *Chesapeake* seemed
to open her sails again, this time in defense of an old inland water
mill, positioning herself in battle to stay alive and overcome the
forces against her, as she had done many times in the past.

In 1997, the vicar of the adjoining village of Shedfield,
Geoffrey Morrell, led the charge. "It is crucial," he wrote in the
introduction to an ambitious proposal, "that we act quickly to
enable this building to be shared as part of our heritage and to be
an important resource for future generations…We hope that you
will want to be part of this significant project of local, national
and international importance." The proposal, by a group of the
movers and shakers of the Meon River Valley, had grown out of
a survey taken in 1995 seeking opinions on how the region ought

The last millstones in use in the Chesapeake Mill. As in *The Domesday Book* of 1086, the value of a mill was tied to the quality and value of its millstones. These stones probably came from a quarry in France, according to John Silman of the Hampshire Mills Group. Valued at twenty-two shillings in 1086, they would probably have a current value of £3,000. *The Chesapeake Mill.*

to celebrate the coming millennium. It sought to convert the mill into an Environmental and Heritage, Visitor and Study Centre that would restore the technologies of water power and support environmentalism. It would teach the history of the valley and of Great Britain and the United States, and it would attract visitors from both countries.

The proposal required the renewal of the mill's credentials as derived from a U.S. Navy frigate, which were provided in an inspection by Brian Lavery, curator of ship technology for the National Maritime Museum in Greenwich. In a letter to the group, he concurred with the known history of the building's timbers, saying that they were formed

> *in the appearance of deck beams and ledges... Timber analysis in the USA* [by the U.S. Forest Service] *shows that the beams were made from a type of timber consistent with forming part of an American ship, not a British one. The beams appear to have been about 14 inches in thickness in their original state, designed to carry quite heavy guns, and as far as I know there was not another American ship as large as this which was broken up in England around this time.*

Two weeks later, the group received a four-sentence letter from the American ambassador in London that, in its brevity and lukewarm quality, would predict the official American response to the mill that would mark the following years. "I found the story," wrote William J. Crowe Jr., "fascinating…You are involved in a very worthwhile endeavor and I wish you the best for its success."

The effort failed, however. An attempt to raise £714,000 to fund the project through a grant from the Heritage Lottery Fund, Britain's largest resource for historic preservation, was not successful.

As the county took possession of the mill, the grass-roots effort to steer the timbers into a safe harbour only increased. Naval historian James Thomas of the University of Portsmouth best summarized what the preservationists were attempting to protect.

> *I see there a substantial structure which at one stage performed very important industrial tasks and this structure is marked by very, very impressive timbers, and I see it as a reflection of the type of technology we used to use, and do not now to anywhere near the same extent—industrial and maritime technology both. You've got to go and look at some of those timbers. I suppose it depends on whether your eye is trained or not, but I look at a structure like that and I think to myself how could people actually select timber, cut it, turn it into a living organism, send it out to sea to defend a new nation. Another nation captures it, reverses the process, breaks it up, sells it and, if you like, the ship ceases to be a living organism.*
>
> *But every time I go down there I get the feeling—maybe it's my identification with the past as a professional historian—I get the impression that there's still something about the soul of the ship that is there.*

Beyond the fact of a ship that became a flour mill, John Wain, of the Britannia Naval Research Association (BNRA), thought that the building could be presented as a dramatic representation of something more profound, pointing to "the folly of war" between two nations so closely related to each other. "The essence of the Special Relationship could be said to be embedded in the mill just as the timbers of *Chesapeake* are. The continuing human interest theme would be the present struggle to save the mill, and the demonstration of how conflict can result in reconciliation. There are many parallels but the *Chesapeake* is unique."

John Wain also saw the mill as a reminder of the mistake that had occurred in 1807. The *Chesapeake/Leopard* incident of 1807 was a "brazen attack on a defenseless ship, we just went ahead and did it—that one incident has spawned the greatest navy we've ever seen…We clearly were out of order." That was not an uncommon view almost two hundred years after the fact. "We Brits were bullying the little Americans," said John Silman of the Hampshire Mills Group. His partner in attempting to save the Chesapeake Mill, Tony Yoward, looked farther back to Revolutionary times. "Nowadays the teaching is that we treated the Americans pretty badly. Let's face it, if we'd behaved ourselves properly and not tried to force the Americans then we would probably still be from the same country."

Hampshire Mills Group was set up in 1970 to research, preserve and teach about the mills of Hampshire. It had seen too many old mills purchased as novelties and turned into something else: condominiums, restaurants, trendy boutiques. Where the Chesapeake Mill was concerned, it saw some of the machinery of an old technology still there to be preserved, and in a building still alive with the sources of its history.

Tony Yoward and John Silman had befriended Bruce Tappenden as he tried to keep his mill alive. "Bruce told me," said Tony Yoward, "he was working in the mill one day and he had occasion to cut into one of the beams, and he said the smell immediately comes out of that timber and you can smell, you could smell the resin in the timber two hundred years after the ship was captured and brought back to Britain."

When the County of Hampshire thinks about itself, it places its assets into the usual categories of business, environment and the people, but it gives equal weight to a historic environment of buildings, farms, churches, schools, ships and forms of architecture, such as Winchester Cathedral, Wolvesey Castle, thatched roofs and the Royal Dockyards. Wickham sits almost twenty miles equidistant between Jane Austen's literary home in Chawton and Charles Dickens's 1812 birthplace at 393 Old Commercial Road in Portsmouth. The goal of the County Council of Hampshire is to preserve that history for its educational value, as much as for tourism. But to Gary Carroll of the county's Department of Estates Practice, the beginning of the Chesapeake's new chapter came at a time of transition in the way Hampshire approached preservation. "We bought it when it was becoming more dilapidated. Leadership of the county at the time wanted to buy and restore historic buildings, and other properties in the same way, and try to find a suitable use for them." A few years later, however, that philosophy would take a more practical course as the council's objectives, driven by government cutbacks in public spending, became more concentrated on core services, such as education, children's and older persons' services.

Apart from the absence of sufficient direct funding, said Gary Carroll, "Officers and Members of the County Council did not believe that an outright museum use was appropriate for the Mill. It had always been a working building." The county's goal was to find a sustainable use for the mill as a commercial operation while restoring and preserving its historic features in a way that would allow good public access.

During that time of transition, archaeological work was begun in earnest at the mill. A November 2002 article in the *Telegraph* was headlined, "Water mill holds secrets of US warship," and offered a debatable judgment on the conversion of the ship to the mill in 1820.

> *As the British prepared to board the USS Chesapeake in 1813 after a short but bloody battle, her captain tried to rally his crew with his dying cry: "Don't give up the boat."*
>
> *The motto may have entered into American folklore but the warship was denied a glorious end. Captured by the British, the pride of the United States fleet was broken up, sold for timber and, in a final insult, used to build a water mill in tranquil Hampshire.*
>
> *Now, nearly 200 years after the Chesapeake's final battle, scientists have returned to her last resting place to unlock her secrets.*

An insult perhaps, but it was one that turned out to be a life preserver for the old warship.

The scientific expedition into the mill was led by Dr. Robert Prescott of the Maritime Studies Institute at the University of St.

The timbers of the USS *Chesapeake* gave atmosphere to a setting of the television miniseries *Master of the Moor*, broadcast on ITV England in 1994. Based on a murder mystery by novelist Ruth Rendell, the series about the serial killing of blonde women on the wild moors was described by one critic as "extremely strange." *The Chesapeake Mill.*

Andrews, Scotland. Adding on to Brian Lavery's earlier assessment of the mill's timbers, he found, among many other things, what he believed to be the initials of William Hughes, the Royal Navy's master shipwright in Halifax, engraved in the wood, possibly denoting points of repair or replacement. "There is a lot of damage," he said, "and a lot of glancing blows which have bruised the timber…We can see where it has been repaired and where a graving piece was used to replace damage."

By that time, the once young Eric Walker was approaching his seventies, fifty of those years lived in Gosport. His lifetime had been spent studying the mill as an avocation, and his later years working on the restoration of the HMS *Warrior*, the Royal Navy's first iron-hulled and armor-plated warship, launched in 1861. Working in relation to the Prescott study, he knew the wood of the old mill well. He had stuck his knife into it to test the resistance that would indicate its age. He thought that some if it held metal deep within that could have been grapeshot gained in battle, or, more simply, the nails that were used in construction. And he knew that a lot of wood built into various structures in the County of Hampshire that was believed to have come from the USS/HMS *Chesapeake* was not from that ship. In some cases, it was taken from an entirely different HMS *Chesapeake*, launched at Chatham Dockyard in 1855, that served in the East Indies and China before breaking in 1867. Portsmouth Cathedral, for example, is built of some of the timbers from the later HMS *Chesapeake*, denoted by an undated brass plate in the church. "Americans come over here," Walker said, "and they see this brass plate, and they say 'Oh, it's from our *Chesapeake*.' And it's not."

As the winds of political change in Hampshire were beginning to stir in 2003, it was Robert Prescott who put down the simple marker: "It is essential that an appropriate and sympathetic new use should be found for this internationally significant mill if it is to survive." That was the county's view, too, but there were differing ideas about how that goal should be reached.

In Wickham itself, the discussion was about commerce versus history. There were those who looked at the mill and saw a restaurant or office condominiums that would realize the worst fears of the Hampshire Mills Group and maritime interests. That kind of use would require plumbing, heating and air conditioning systems that would cut into timbers, and walls and floors that would cover the old channels and trapdoors through which the grains had traveled on their way from raw to refined. It did not help that from the town's perspective, the mill had always been something

of a mystery. Its origins were generally known, but never greatly appreciated in the press of business. And perhaps it was perceived as a structure that was not as much a part of the town as it was of somewhere else.

Barrie Marson and the History Society represented the mill in the deliberations about its future as the quiet but powerful thing that it was, "a valuable symbol of the history of our two countries. When you explain it to people, very few people know about it. It comes as an enormous surprise to most people that we were at war with the United States in 1812."

And he held it up against the remains of another war, the one that everyone old enough still remembered, often with great emotion. It was from the airfields of east England that the U.S. Eighth Air Force bombardment wings had taken off in the missions against German factories and rail lines in World War II. They would become known in popular culture through the book, movie and television series *Twelve O'Clock High*.

"I try to compare the mill," said Marson, "with similar connections. Just south of Cambridge is the American Cemetery with those Air Force people. That is a real place of pilgrimage; thousands of Americans go there every year. They read the history of the U.S. Air Force between 1942 and 1945." Indeed, the

An aerial view of Chesapeake Mill, circa 1980s. The Meon River flows beneath Bridge Street between the mill and mill house. Market Square sits one hundred meters to the west (left, out of the view of the picture) at the end of Bridge Street. Bridge Street becomes Southwick Road to the east, leading to the planning site of the Normandy invasion. *The Chesapeake Mill.*

Cambridge cemetery held 3,812 American dead. The Brookwood American Cemetery, adjacent to Hampshire in Surrey County, held 468 Americans. They were places of pilgrimage.

Cemeteries were powerful pieces of land, and it turned out that the wake of the USS *Chesapeake* had left behind a shared cemetery of its own.

CHAPTER 6

THE LOST CEMETERY

At the same time that the fate of the Chesapeake Mill in Wickham
was being debated in England, Guy MacLean—professor of
history, president emeritus of Mt. Allison University and retired
vice-president of Dalhousie University in Halifax—learned of
plans to place a condominium development on a lonely piece of
waterfront land on the Northwest Arm of Halifax Harbour. The
Arm was one of the most beautiful pieces of residential Halifax,
lined with large houses and green spaces. Its water sparkled when
Halifax was favored by the sun. The yachts and sailboats of the
Armdale Yacht Club bobbed and swayed in a safe harbour just a
few miles from the open Atlantic. Armdale's clubhouse sat across
a cove from a green space at the foot of a small, deeply wooded
hill known as Deadman's Island, the proposed site of the new
condominiums.

Guy Maclean had also been Nova Scotia's official ombudsman for
five years. The purpose of the office was to provide "independent,
unbiased investigations into complaints against provincial and
municipal government departments, agencies, boards and
commissions." Guy MacLean knew how to work for desired
outcomes, and he started a campaign against the condominiums.
Though a historian, he did not yet know how the power of history
would become his ally. It was a history that, once again, started
with timbers.

Halifax is a peninsula, and was named by its early native tribes
Gwoarmiktook, "the place of great white pines." As the earliest
settlers came to Halifax in the eighteenth century, the first known
sawmill appeared near the Arm in 1752, and the pine, maple, oak
and beech trees became the construction materials of the growing
town, its buildings and furniture. Work and settlement along the
Arm was fueled by the tidal waters that brought the freshest of
food, and the occasional lost whale, from the nearby Atlantic.

When the British settlement of Nova Scotia was begun in
earnest in 1749 under Governor Edward Cornwallis, a subsequent

The residence of Premier Edgar Nelson Rhodes on the Northwest Arm, Halifax, 1928. *Canada Science and Technology Museum.*

Many prisoners kept animals. Some had hens, housed in cabins made of stone and earth that were located in the prison yard, that fed on scraps. Some had pigs. One man had raised a kitten that danced like a monkey and meowed at its master's command. This cat always slept with its master.
—from the journal of Francois Lambert Bourneuf, Melville Island prisoner from 1809 until his escape in 1811

exploration of the Northwest Arm revealed a small island that would come to embody the often tragic human dimension of the history that was to follow. It was used at first by private owners for fisheries and timber operations, but as Halifax developed as a base for British operations in the 1790s, the need for prison space to accommodate captured French sailors led to the conversion of fishing stores on the island to a prison hospital for seventy inmates. In 1803, the British formally purchased the four-acre island and named it after the newly appointed first lord of the admiralty Henry Dundas, Viscount Melville.

It was with the first Spanish and French prisoners that Melville Island would take a curious place in the life of the larger, tolerant Halifax community. The detention barracks were uncomfortable places, but life for most prisoners on the island was one of fishing and drinking spruce beer. French prisoners, in particular, were given leeway to work in the larger community. Those prisoners who had come from the trades—tailors, shoemakers, masons, jewelers, schoolteachers, even actors—were allowed to enter their services into the general labor pool. Shops, entertainments and gambling opportunities were set up on the prison grounds, which were visited on the weekends by wealthy Haligonians who came by boat or walked across the ice in the winter.

But, with all of its delights, Melville Island was still a prison. As the years went on, it became a more uncomfortable and unhealthy place. As prisoners continued to try to escape, it became more secure. Floggings took place, and the internal policing methods of prisoner groups could be quick and brutal. Informant inmates known within their peer group were occasionally stoned to death

Melville Island
Prison, circa 1800s.
*Halifax Citadel
National Historic Site
of Canada.*

off the books. The worst official offenses would result in time spent alone with bread and water in the Black Hole, essentially the prison's basement. And when prisoners died, for whatever reason, they were likely taken for burial in an anonymous cemetery on the other side of the cove.

The advent of the War of 1812 pressed hard on living conditions in the prison, and created a much more restrictive lifestyle for newly arrived Americans than had been enjoyed by the French. Halifax would become an active center of the trading of international prisoners. Groups of the captured would come and go based on differing rates of exchange between various ranks and nationalities. They would be repatriated in some cases, sent on to the dreaded Dartmoor Prison in England in others or fated to serve out the war in Halifax. The work of Melville Island was supplemented by the prison hulks in the harbour, but as the war progressed it became badly overcrowded.

A number of firsthand accounts of life on Melville Island exist. Among the most widely known is from the 1815 *Journal of a Young Man of Massachusetts*. It is written in the name of Benjamin Waterhouse, "a surgeon on board an American privateer captured first by the British May, 1813 and was confined first at Melville Island." It is believed, however, that the journal, though deemed historically accurate, is a compendium of wide-ranging firsthand accounts of the War of 1812 obtained and edited by Waterhouse under his name.

In his real life, Waterhouse was one of the first three faculty members of Harvard Medical School, and was the first American

On this nauseous spot is situated a building of two stories, one hundred and thirty feet in length by forty broad, and of the upper room thirty feet is set apart for the sick. The remainder of this apartment now contains one hundred and eighty American prisoners. In the lower room are seven hundred and seventy more, cooped up to breathe the same air and generate diseases by this narrow confine. Three hundred and fifty more are near this island in a prison ship…they are told by the British agent, Miller, "to die and be damned, the king has one hundred and fifty acres of land to bury them in."

—A History of American Privateers, Edgar MacLay, 1900

doctor to test a smallpox vaccine, doing so on his family. Against much resistance, he persisted in distributing the vaccine. His campaign enlisted Thomas Jefferson as a believer in the cause, and Jefferson began giving it to native tribes in 1802. Waterhouse presented an original copy of the *Journal of a Young Man* to Jefferson as a gift.

In the journal, the narrator describes capture by the British and a two-mile march through Halifax to the boat to Melville Island. At the prison gates, names were called and new arrivals were given hammocks and blankets. Inside, they were immediately set upon by other prisoners for news of the outside world. The narrator described the long nights:

> *The general hum and confused noise from almost every hammock was, at first, very distressing. Some would be lamenting their hard fate at being shut up like Negro slaves in a guinea ship, or like fowls in a hen coop, for no crime, but for fighting the battles of their country. Some were cursing and execrating their oppressors; others, late at night, were relating their adventures to a new prisoner; others lamenting their disobedience to parents, and head-strong willfulness, that drove them to sea, contrary to their parents wish, while others of the younger class were sobbing out their lamentations at what their mothers and sisters suffered at the knowledge of their imprisonment. Not infrequently, the whole night was spent in this way, and when, about day break, the weary prisoner fell into a doze, he was wracked from his slumber by the winding noise of the locks, and the unbarring of the doors, with the cry "turn out—all out" when each man took down his hammock and lashed it up, and slung it on his back, and was ready to answer the roll-call of the turnkey.*

Many accounts of Melville Island tell of a curious inhumanity. Every two weeks, all prisoners were ordered out of the barracks so that the floors could be swept and washed. No one was allowed to reenter until they were dry. Especially in the harsh winters of Nova Scotia, that could take a long time while the inmates stood outside in the barest of clothing, often in sub-zero temperatures.

The world within the prison, because of the constant comings and goings of its inmates, was fairly aware of the events of the war. The British view of the War of 1812, Waterhouse's narrator learned from his jailers, was of "an unhappy strife between brethren; and they all attribute this 'unnatural war' to a French influence…all the odium of the war ought to fall on our [American] administration and their wicked seducers, the French."

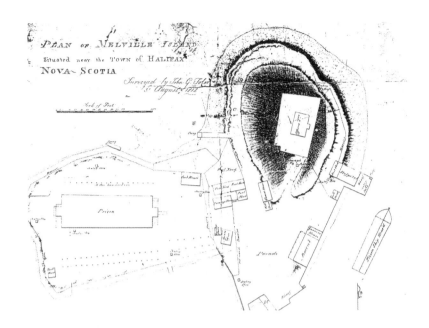

A survey of Melville Island, August 31, 1812. The prison is on the east side, and a prison hulk sits offshore to the west.

The fate of James Lawrence in the battle between the *Chesapeake* and the *Shannon* was widely discussed. "Early in the month of July, we were not a little disturbed by the arrival of the crew of our ill-omened, ill-fated *Chesapeake*." What the *Chesapeake* sailors may have said about that event is not reported, but the narrator reflects an anguish about James Lawrence and the *Chesapeake* that would linger in American naval history. Referring to Lawrence's decision to place a full military uniform and hat on his easily targeted six-foot, four-inch frame in preparation for the battle, he wrote, "No one doubted his bravery, but some have called his prudence into question…The name of Lawrence is consecrated in America while his ever unlucky ship is doomed to everlasting ignominy." That ignominy was a reference to the 1807 *Chesapeake/Leopard* affair, still fresh in American memory, and the following referred to her encounter with the *Shannon*: "From all that I could gather she was not judiciously brought into action, nor well fought after Lawrence fell."

Like hundreds of others, Waterhouse's narrator was eventually moved to Dartmoor Prison in England, those transports taking place on British warships returning home. The HMS *Chesapeake* is reported to have been one of them, traveling in August 1814, a month after she had been sighted in the Chesapeake Bay. Compared to Dartmoor, the Melville Island prison had been easy time in a splendid harbour. After a long and brutal march from Plymouth Harbour to the county of Devon,

We came in sight of the black, bleak, and barren moor, without a solitary bush or blade of grass. Some of our prisoners swore that we had marched the whole length of England and got into Scotland. We all agreed that it was not credible that such a hideous, barren spot could be any where found in England…The moment we entered the dark prison we found ourselves jammed in with a multitude; one calling us to come this way, another that; some halloing, swearing and cursing, so that I did not know, for a moment, but what I had died through fatigue and hard usage, and was actually in the regions of the damned. Oh, what a horrid night I here passed! The floors of this reproach to Old England were of stone, damp and mouldy, and smelling like a transport. Here we had to lay down and sleep after a most weary march of fifteen miles. What apology can be made for not having things prepared for our comfort?

The young man's journal, one of its major story lines the brutality of British imprisonment, concludes with his safe return, in tears, to New York City on June 7, 1815. And it adds a postscript for all times:

If the present race of Britons have not become indifferent to a sense of national character, their government will take measures to wipe off the stain from her garments. Let the nations of Europe inquire how the Americans treat their prisoners of war. If we treat them with barbarity publish our disgrace to the wide world, and speak of us accordingly, let them, at the same time, inquire how the English treated those of us who have had the great misfortune of falling into their hands; and let them be spoken of accordingly. My serious opinion is, that this little book will aid the great cause of humanity.

Another of the prisoners who later passed through Melville Island was James Fenimore Cooper's friend Ned Myers. Myers had grown up in Halifax but ran away to sea at a young age, hidden in the cargo of potatoes of an American schooner. He would eventually return to Halifax as an American prisoner. In Cooper's *Ned Myers; or, a life before the mast*, published in 1856, Myers recounted an intriguing story of the life of a sailor in the wars, and of the ghosts of existence that life could create. He told of a time at Melville Island when his sister, whom he had left behind as a runaway boy, came to the prison gate with some knowledge that he might be in residence.

In the forest of graves on Target Hill. *Courtesy of the author.*

Go view the graves which prisoners fill
Go count them on the rising hill
No Monumental marble shows
Whose silent dust does there repose
Save that the Papal cross is placed
Next to the graves where papist rest
All sleep unknown; their bodies rot
By all, save distant friends forgot
–from a poem composed by a prisoner on
Melville Island, in *The Diary of Benjamin F.
Palmer a Privateersman*

I refused to go to the gate, however, to see who it was, and Jack [a friend] *was sent back to tell the woman that I had been left behind at Bermuda. He was directed to throw in a few hints about the expediency of her not coming back to look for me, and that it would be better if she never named me. All this was done, I getting a berth from which I could see the female. I knew her in a moment, although she was married, and had a son with her, and my heart was very near giving way, especially when I saw her shedding tears. She went away from the gate, however, going up on the ramparts, from which she could look down into the prison-yard. There she remained an hour, as if she wished to satisfy her own eyes as to the truth of Jack's story; but I took good care to keep out of her sight.*

The end of the War of 1812 closed a chapter in the history of Melville Island that, in sheer numbers, reflected the forces at play in the Atlantic community. From 1803 to 1813, 1,535 French prisoners were recorded as having passed through the prison, with just 56 of them left behind in the anonymous graveyard across the cove, by now called Target Hill. Of an unknown number of Spanish prisoners in 1805, 9 were taken to the graveyard, which accepted 10 more French in 1814. But it was the Americans, 8,148 of them, who mostly populated Melville Island. They were drawn from the battles on the ocean, on land and in the Great Lakes. Of these prisoners, 188 would be left behind in the mass graveyard, 11 of them recorded as sailors of the USS *Chesapeake*.

That chapter closed, another was immediately opened. The last years of the war, and the following years, saw a rapid immigration into Halifax of American slaves escaped mostly from Virginia on the lower Chesapeake Bay. It was a movement encouraged by the British, who had begun to abolish their own practices of slavery in 1807. The word was put out in the coastal areas of the South that British ships would transport those seeking to escape their bondage either to the West Indies or to British North America. They would be gainfully employed in the dockyards and enlisted in battle against the Americans. An estimated two thousand were brought to Halifax and were accepted into the city in the spirit of its usual openness.

Many arrived, however, at the time of a smallpox epidemic. Those who needed it were given medical care at the city's poorhouse, but their numbers increased, and the decision was made to turn the prison into a hospital. Its walls and floors were whitewashed, its windows and doors were repaired and it took in perhaps 100 refugees, though without a strength of shelter to fully protect the former residents of the American South from the brutal winter of 1816 on the Northwest Arm. The immigration would result in 1,600 former slaves remaining to become ancestors of modern-day blacks in Nova Scotia, 107 of them laid to rest in the soils of Target Hill.

After that, the island and its buildings fell into disuse, but only for a time. In 1829, Nova Scotia historian Thomas Chandler

Haliburton visited the place. "All the buildings," he wrote, "are in a state of neglect and decay; a wooden bridge connects the island with the main land, and on a small hill to the southward is the burying ground belonging to the establishment. It is now no longer to be distinguished from the surrounding woods, but by the mounds of earth that have been placed over the dead; the whole being covered with a thick shrubbery of forest trees."

As the century wore on, Halifax was called upon again to give shelter to the casualties of the larger world. Increasingly, the movement of immigrants on the Atlantic brought the desperate, and often sick, to the city's wharves. Into the 1840s, Melville Island served as the hospital for newly arrived diseased. In a smallpox epidemic, those not yet infected were given the vaccine developed by Benjamin Waterhouse, and those beyond help were collected by the overgrown graveyard. Then, in 1847, refugees began to arrive from the Irish potato famine, bringing typhus to the city, and were treated at the island hospital. The cemetery claimed thirty-seven more as its own.

Years passed. In 1907, the symbiotic relationship between Melville Island and its burial ground, now known as Deadman's Island, was continued in a different way. Melville, which had housed the British Foreign Legion in 1855 (a failed attempt to recruit Americans into service in the Crimean War) and served as a British military prison until 1905, continued as a place of military detention in newly built, and more comfortable, stone barracks. Surrounding properties in the Northwest Arm, including Deadman's Island, came under the ownership of a developer who built cottages and a dance pavilion on the shoreline, and turned the old cemetery into an amusement park of sorts. Children frolicked on the playground equipment of the day, dances and sporting events were held and sodas and ice cream were consumed.

Occasionally, though, the island's past as a repository of an estimated four hundred anonymous graves would show itself. As in a few occasions in the late nineteenth century, skeletal remains would reveal themselves after a particularly hard rain, for example. The new owner of the property came across three skulls while digging a berry patch and put them on display at the pavilion, but they were eventually stolen. The occasional appearance of human bones, newly emerged from the soil, would continue into the late twentieth century.

The commercial venture on the Arm eventually failed, just as Halifax began once again to play its role in the hardships of the larger world. In 1912 the city, its citizens of every stripe, its

Of the victims of the sinking of the *Titanic*, 121 were buried in Fairview Cemetery, Halifax (shown); 19 victims believed to be Catholic were buried in Mount Olivet Catholic Cemetery, and 10 are in the Baron de Hirsch Jewish Cemetery. The City of Halifax maintains perpetual care for all of the *Titanic* graves. *Frances J. Beck.*

churches, hospitals and mortuaries had mobilized themselves in response to the sinking of the RMS *Titanic* off the Grand Banks of Newfoundland. The ship's passengers included the wealthy of England and France, and the less well off of Ireland, mostly in steerage. Those survivors in good condition were taken on to New York, but it fell to the Halifax-based *MacKay-Bennett* to tend to the dead. She left the harbour on April 17 with a supply of pine coffins, clergy and undertakers. Identifiable bodies were taken aboard, and the unidentifiable were returned to the sea in ceremony. More than a week later, the *MacKay-Bennett* and a sister ship had recovered 306 bodies, including that of the millionaire John Jacob Astor, and returned 116 to the sea.

Much as they had when the *Shannon* had brought the *Chesapeake* into the harbour in 1813, the Haligonians watched as the *MacKay-Bennett* pulled up to wharves stacked with coffins and the dead were brought ashore. Memorial services were held in the churches, and, once again, Halifax took the refugees of the sea into its care.

Then came World War I. The city was the main base of a new Canadian navy, and the warships, troop and supply ships of the Allied Powers crowded the wharves. It was here that convoys were formed before heading east into the Atlantic.

On December 6, 1917, the harbour became the setting of what has been called the largest man-made explosion known to history up to that time, only dwarfed since by the atomic bomb explosion over Hiroshima in 1945. At 8:45 a.m., a Belgian vessel collided

William Waldorf Astor, cousin to John Jacob Astor, purchased the last U.S. flag of the USS *Chesapeake* for $4,250 and presented it to the United Service Institution of Great Britain. It was displayed in their museum at Whitehall, London. This photograph is dated January 1914. *U.S. Naval Historical Center.*

with a French munitions ship, the *Mont Blanc*. Fire on the French ship intensified as she drifted toward the city wharves. Knowing what was to come, those crew members of the *Mont Blanc* who could do so rowed to the shores of Halifax and across the harbour to Dartmouth to warn onlookers to run for cover. The explosion of the munitions ship was said to have been heard one hundred miles away on Prince Edward Island. Damage and fires extended to a one-mile radius from the ship, and a huge wave of water reached onto the shores of Halifax and Dartmouth, pulling onlookers back into the harbour. More than 1,900 people were killed and 9,000 injured; 1,600 buildings were destroyed, and 12,000 houses were damaged. More than 30,000 people were left homeless or with inadequate shelter. The following day saw the advent of the worst blizzard recorded in Halifax, and it continued for a week. Help began to arrive from the rest of the world immediately. Funerals went on for weeks.

One of twelve thousand houses damaged in the Halifax explosion of 1917. *Library of Congress.*

The event imprinted itself indelibly in the history and the soul of the city that seemed always to be sitting quietly at the center of the Western world, especially when that world fell into disarray. And with the explosion, Halifax, rather than retreating with its wounds, once again became an example for others. In reaction to the tragedy, international maritime treaties and standards were changed and the management of safer harbors and the worldwide movement of dangerous materials were improved. Emergency Measures Organizations (EMOs) were developed. Emergency medicine and psychological services had to be developed on the spot, and came to be modeled internationally. Standards of practice and equipment for emergency response by disparate entities were developed.

Another result was that as Canada fell into a postwar recession, Halifax boomed with reconstruction and the opportunity to redesign itself in positive ways. The buildings on Melville Island, however, had reverted to their original purposes as detention barracks for the Canadian military. At the outset of World War II, those buildings that had not been destroyed in previous fires became munitions stores. The chief warder's house, built before the outbreak of the War of 1812, was still standing as a residence for island caretakers. The graveyard of the small peninsula known as Deadman's Island had disappeared into the forest once again.

Eventually, the warder's house, the longest standing original building on Melville Island, became the clubhouse of the Armdale Yacht Club, and it was there that Guy MacLean attended a meeting

Halifax, circa 1935. The streetcar starts its ride down Barrington Street. The first stand of trees on the west side of Barrington Street rises above the Old Burying Ground, and the following steeples are of St. Mary's Basilica and St. Paul's Church. The citadel overlooks the city and its harbour. *Canada Science and Technology Museum.*

of the Northwest Arm Heritage Association in February of 1998. The clubhouse was overflowing with very concerned residents and others. A land development company had gained possession of Deadman's Island, and proposed to build a sixty-condominium structure on one of the last undeveloped spaces of the Northwest Arm. Its parking garage would be placed in a hollowed-out section of Target Hill.

Heritage members and others in Halifax were, in the word of historian Iris Shea, "appalled." Unsuccessful efforts to develop the island had come up before. In 1966, Nova Scotia historian and author Thomas Raddall published the novel *Hangman's Beach*, modeled after Melville Island and its graveyard, and proposed that Deadman's Island be declared a national historic site, to no avail. The problem seems to have been that, though there was a general consciousness of the cemetery's history, the specifics of its burials were elusive and incomplete. The initial planning of those who opposed the condominium project was based on arguments that were more contemporary than historic: the preservation of green space and mitigation of environmental damage to the Arm.

The day after the meeting, Iris Shea, also a genealogical researcher and community historian, sent a casual e-mail to a fellow researcher in the United States, a military man. She told him what was planned for the cemetery, in which it was vaguely known that American casualties of war were buried. "Well, I guess not!" was his firm response. He contacted other military organizations and interests to seek their support in saving the island, receiving a tepid response at first. But as Guy MacLean began to gain a further

A portion of the admiralty records of those buried on Deadman's Island. *U.S. National Archives.* A full transcribed list of those from the USS *Chesapeake* can be seen on page 119.

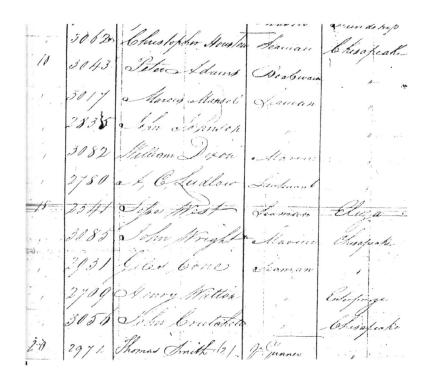

understanding of the nature and numbers of the burials, his talking points became obvious. "Would we dig up the *Titanic* graves for a housing project?" he asked a conference on the future of the municipality's parks and wilderness areas. He suggested that Nova Scotians would be outraged if housing were built over their war dead in Boston, for example.

One day, Iris Shea was speaking to a colleague at the Nova Scotia Archives and Records Management (NSARM) in Halifax, and told him about the situation on the Northwest Arm. "As a matter of fact," he said, "we just received something that might be of interest to you."

The British had kept meticulous records during the War of 1812; meticulous, but layered upon by other meticulous records, most of them eventually lost in memory and filing systems, if not in fact. But for some reason, just at the time that both the Chesapeake Mill in Wickham and Deadman's Island in Halifax were in danger of becoming condominium developments, or something similar in the case of the mill, there emerged from the admiralty records in London a list of everyone who had been buried on Deadman's Island between 1803 and 1815. Sent to the U.S. National Archive on microfilm, it included the names, battle units or ships, hometowns, ages and causes of death of 195 Americans, 188 of whom were probably buried on the island.

At that moment Guy MacLean knew that Deadman's Island would be saved by the force of history. He knew that actual names and vital information about Americans buried in the forested hill would gain the necessary attention of American interests to the south. His parents had been New Englanders, and much of his family remained in the United States, where he had earned his doctorate degree. It was important to him that an American burial site be preserved, and it was also information that he could use. Up until then, an archaeologist working for the developer had suggested that the bones that could be found on the land were those of anonymous individuals, and could be respected by a work-around in construction. As bones of identifiable Americans, however, they could, themselves, exert considerable political leverage. Guy Maclean spoke of those buried on Deadman's Island in human terms. "No doubt their loved ones wept, for they seemed to have vanished from the memory of the United States," was a line most often quoted in newspaper accounts of the events.

The names given to those buried who had been crew members of the USS *Chesapeake* were transcribed from admiralty records by Michele Hovey Raymond of Halifax:

Christopher Houster, seaman, born unknown, age unknown,
    Died June 7, 1813 of wounds received
Peter Adams, boatswain, born unknown, age 42,
    Died June 6, 1813 of wounds received
Marcus Mansel, seaman, born Sweden, age 22,
    Died June 11, 1813 of wounds received
John Johnson, seaman, born New York, age 22
    Died June 12, 1813 of wounds received
William Dixon, seaman, born unknown, age unknown,
    Died June 13, 1813 of wounds received
A.C. Ludlow, rank unknown, born unknown, age unknown,
    Died June 13, 1813 of wounds received
John Wright, marine, born Pennsylvania, age 22,
    Died June 14, 1813 of wounds received
Giles Corle, seaman, born Middle Town, age 30,
    Died June 15, 1813 of wounds received
John Crutchet, seaman, born Cumberland, age 34,
    Died June 20, 1813 of wounds received
Thomas Smith (?), gunner, born Hampton, age 22
    Died July 13, 1813 cause unnoted
John Carleton, seaman, born Boston, age 26,
    Died October 9, 1813 of pneumonia

Also Left Behind

When the Harnish family of Hubbards, Nova Scotia, needed a new feed trough for its dairy farm in 1813, it bought the *Chesapeake*'s cooking pot at an auction in Halifax. In 1936, Guy Harnish set about to create a large lobster supper on Hubbards Beach, cleaned up the old pot and put it in service. His efforts led to the opening of the Shore Club dance hall by Roy Harnish in 1946, and the *Chesapeake*'s old cooking pot was used for lobster until 1957. It was estimated to have cooked one million lobsters in its time, and is now on exhibit at the Maritime Museum of the Atlantic in Halifax. The Shore Club continued to serve music and lobster into the twenty-first century.

These members of the *Chesapeake* crew are known to be buried at Dartmoor Prison Cemetery in England:

Benjamin Cook, seaman, of Baltimore, Maryland
Died April 6, 1814

Charles Cornish, seaman, of Maryland
Died January 10, 1814

Francis Romel, seaman, of San Sebastian
Died February 7, 1815

At the same time that anonymous bones became real people, the search for an American partner in saving the cemetery got a hit. Letters and messages had been sent to the major national newspapers, veterans' organizations, the Smithsonian Institution, congressmen and the U.S. Army Military History Institute, among others, but it was finally the War of 1812 Society of Ohio that picked up the cause, and with a vengeance.

> *WHEREAS—The Society of the War of 1812 in the State of Ohio feels that any desecration of this sacred place would dishonor the memory of these patriots.*
>
> *WHEREAS—The Society of the War of 1812 in the State of Ohio believes that this cemetery should be properly marked by the United States government.*
>
> *THEREFORE—BE IT RESOLVED this Tenth day of July, 1999 that The Society of the War of 1812 in the State of Ohio requests that the United States be actively involved in the preservation of this island where American servicemen gave the supreme sacrifice and that a suitable monument be erected thereon.*

> *E. Paul Morehouse*
> *President*

The resolution, and the strong sentiments behind it, went forth to any possible American source of support, and, perhaps more importantly for the moment, back to the mayor and city council of Halifax. That importuning from the United States was increasingly complimented by the growing understanding in Halifax of what was at stake. In addition to the site's importance to black Nova Scotians, as the resting place of many of their ancestors, the newly realized mix of international residents of Deadman's Island brought the critical mass of support for its preservation as a city park. When Mayor Walter Fitzgerald, a former history student of Professor Guy MacLean at Dalhousie University, was told of his own affinity with some of those buried in Target Hill, he was quoted in a local newspaper as spluttering, "Irish? I'll tell you for sure we're going to do it now."

In a more thoughtful statement, after the developers had willingly sold the land back to the city for $230,000, less than half its presumed value, Mayor Fitzgerald talked to the *Boston Globe* for a front-page story on May 12, 2000: "They deserve some honor," he said of those buried, "some respect, some memory. The Americans died for their country in our prison. The blacks died seeking freedom. The Irish died looking for a new life in a New World. There's a lot of our North American history on that bit of land."

The *New York Times*, lured to Halifax by Guy MacLean, was the first to put the story into the national press of the United States, and it quoted the mayor on a more practical level. Tourism was a $500 million business in his 250-year-old city. He noted the tour buses that made pilgrimage to the graves of those lost in the sinking of the *Titanic*. "With the number of American tourists coming into Nova Scotia, Deadman's Island could be part of the tour."

Thus the green space on the Northwest Arm had been saved, history had been given its due and the city had once again given of itself to the larger world, with the potential benefit to the bottom line not unnoticed.

But those who had saved Deadman's Island were yet to realize the human dimension of what they had accomplished. That would come with a late-night phone call in June of 2000, culminating in a solemn act of memorial on Canadian soil by a group of American military members. It would remind Guy MacLean of the power of remembrance. It would take modern Halifax back to its historic place at the center of the Atlantic community. And it would mark the return of the USS *Chesapeake* as the emblematic symbol of a past that was newly rediscovered.

CHAPTER 7

THE SOULS OF A SHIP

The 200th anniversary of the USS *Constitution* was celebrated with a short sailing across Boston Harbor in October 1997. The 200th birthday of the USS *Chesapeake*, two years later, went unremarked upon, of course. She had been forgotten in history up until then, and when events in England and Canada began to return her to life at the beginning of her third century, she was still something in which two nations shared a provenance. Another nation, Canada, seemed to hold her in its heart, but none of them owned her in a legal sense. And the whole arc of her story—up the American coast, through Halifax and across the Atlantic to England—was one of a ghost ship: there, but not there; venerated, but ridiculed; bereft of identity, but still identifiable; still an orphan of sorts.

Long after the *Chesapeake* had been launched by the U.S. Naval Shipyard at Gosport, Virginia, the yard was still struggling with its own identity. Corey Thornton is curator of the Portsmouth Naval Shipyard Museum, which celebrates a Portsmouth shipyard actually named the Norfolk Naval Shipyard. It was able to keep its Gosport name until the Civil War when, under the Confederate flag, it gave birth to the ironclad CSS *Virginia* (formerly the USS *Merrimack*), but was virtually burned to the waterline by fleeing Confederate forces. History tells us that when the shipyard was taken by successful Federal forces, it was renamed the United States Navy Yard at Norfolk, ostensibly because there was already a naval shipyard at Portsmouth, New Hampshire, and duplicates would be confusing.

Corey Thornton compares historic outsider attitudes about the *Chesapeake* to the shipyard that gave her life. "It's never been in Norfolk; it's in Portsmouth, which beginning around 1800 has always been a little smaller than Norfolk." Until the Civil War, the Gosport Shipyard was known as the "Workshop of the South," one of the largest shipyards in the country, and the largest in the South.

A monument to the battle of the American *Chesapeake* and the British *Shannon* overlooks the entrance to the Canadian harbour of Halifax. An engraving at Point Pleasant Park says, in part, "Confidence in the British Navy faltered early in the War of 1812 when American vessels won several single-ship engagements. This pattern was broken on June 1, 1813 when HMS Shannon, commanded by Captain Philip Broke, closed with USS Chesapeake under Captain James Lawrence off Boston harbour. The latter was taken in a short and bloody fight, and brought into Halifax by her captor on June 6." *Courtesy of the author.*

"There is that odd-duck feeling. It's hard to put your finger on. It's kind of nestled away down this little river that's pretty narrow. I just watched the [aircraft carrier] USS *Roosevelt* leaving the shipyard this morning. And, boy, it almost devoured the Elizabeth River."

At the beginning of the twenty-first century, Portsmouth, Virginia, is a small, relatively poor city that has recently begun to rediscover the power of its history in ways that can help to secure its better future. Its maritime heritage is increasingly reflected in the signs and symbols of a working waterfront. Its downtown streets are regaining life with restaurants and interesting shops, and its Olde Town houses, some as old as the city itself, are increasingly prized possessions.

In 2007, the Naval Shipyard Museum put up a small exhibit on Portsmouth's important contributions to the founding of the new nation. The exhibit put the story of the USS *Chesapeake* right at its center. "Every locality has events occur that are specific to its own history," said the museum curator, "but sometimes, events come along that make a national connection, and make the general population stand up and say 'Wow!'" It is the museum's job, Corey Thornton believes, to bring people to those "Aha!" moments, and to help them know the historic importance of their own communities.

Occasionally in Portsmouth, people talk about trying to revert their shipyard to its original identity by naming it once again in honor of "God's safe harbour" or the "Port of Geese," from which it sprang in England.

Federal forces set the Gosport Yard afire, rather than giving it up to Virginia troops, on April 20, 1861. Surviving was the Western Hemisphere's first granite dry dock, built in 1833, a national historic landmark in the twenty-first century and still in use. *The Mariners' Museum, Newport News, Virginia.*

The aircraft carrier USS *America* moves toward the Norfolk Naval Shipyard, July 8, 1992, after a cruise in support of United Nations sanctions against Iraq. *Kirn Library, Norfolk, Sargeant Memorial Room.*

Less than three hundred miles north of Portsmouth, another community seeks to define itself in the wake of the *Chesapeake*. Not long after he was buried in Halifax in 1813, Captain James Lawrence was disinterred and eventually laid to rest in Trinity Churchyard on lower Broadway in Manhattan. He was buried a third time when his original and ornate grave marker crumbled, and the church removed his remains in 1848 to a brown freestone mausoleum, with a twenty-first-century view of the American Stock Exchange. His is the most ostentatious of graves in a cemetery that also holds a number of the luminaries of American history and industry: Robert Fulton, Alexander Hamilton and his son Phillip, various signers of the Constitution, senators, writers and John Jacob Astor, late of the RMS *Titanic*.

Lawrence's birthplace is not far away in Burlington, New Jersey, close to the Delaware River and ten miles west of Exit 6 on the New Jersey Turnpike. The attached houses that gave life both to Lawrence and James Fenimore Cooper are pretty much still what they were in the late 1700s, unspoiled by the usual trappings and

The modern harbor sailing ship *American Rover* sails the Elizabeth River toward the Portsmouth waterfront. It offers the chance to gauge the size of the USS *Chesapeake* in this harbor at her launch in 1799. Length: *American Rover* 135 feet; USS *Chesapeake* 152 feet, 6 inches. Beam: *American Rover* 24 feet; USS *Chesapeake* 41 feet. *City of Portsmouth.*

graphics of a modern museum. Like Portsmouth, the town of Burlington is one of those very historic places in America that has not been allowed to rest on its historic laurels. It has had to deal with the economic and social pressures that beset many small towns and old cities.

"Burlington has a great past," said Jeff Macechak, education director of the Burlington County Historical Society. "People should know that it was more than the backwater it is today. It was an important place."

In an alter ego, Jeff Macechak is New Jersey's reenactor of James Lawrence. Though not very close to Lawrence's six-foot, four-inch stature, he has an enthusiasm combined with a no-nonsense edge that might have matched the temperament of the naval captains of Lawrence's time. He has traveled to Wickham and received inspiration from the timbers of Chesapeake Mill. His view of the force of history and its particulars is direct and timeless.

Of Lawrence, Decatur, Barron, Broke, Wallis and the others he said, "They were the astronauts of their time, the Lindberghs. All were about the same age, friends that knew each other. They were an elite little crew. They did the same kind of thing, and were special. The Americans and British were part of that same club. They would capture each other, have dinner together, and pass the time of day with a lot of grace."

Through Jeff Macechak, James Lawrence is a constant presence in Burlington. Children gather around the young naval captain in the schools. He is a guest of honor in parades and Fourth of July picnics. But Jeff Macechak knows that, outside of Burlington, James Lawrence is not as revered in the United States as he is in other countries. He thinks it ironic that Lawrence's career was established by his work with Stephen Decatur in the Tripolitan War ("They were like the Navy Seals of today"), which in turn led him to become a judge on James Barron's court-martial onboard the *Chesapeake*, which eventually led him to command of that "sort of a cursed ship."

But "Lawrence was a revered figure in Halifax. His battle with the *Peacock*, before the *Shannon*, was a great victory. He was considered, like the Red Baron, the guy to get, and treated with respect when they got him. He should be honored. It was like shooting down the Red Baron."

He was a very generous, lenient man, said his reenactor. In terms of modern culture, he was not Errol Flynn, but more like Russell Crowe, and most certainly a model for novelist Patrick O'Brian's hero Jack Aubrey in the Aubrey/Maturin novels. Aubrey was

The mausoleum of James Lawrence in Trinity Churchyard, Manhattan, circa 1848. *Naval Shipyard Museum, Portsmouth, Virginia.*

Captain James Lawrence/Jeffrey Macechak presides in full uniform over Fourth of July festivities in 2007 on the Delaware River at Riverton, New Jersey. One of his crew is portrayed by Eric Pfeiffer. *Burlington County Historical Society.*

played by Crowe in the film *Master and Commander: The Far Side of the World*. And indeed, the *Chesapeake/Shannon* battle brings the O'Brian novel *The Fortune of War* to its conclusion.

In Burlington there is a Lawrence Street, of course, and a Lawrence Elementary School where the children are often surprised to learn that their school is named after a real person who they can study and know about. "Don't Give Up the Ship" is the town motto, chiseled over the doorway of the old city hall that has since turned into an arts center. On Burlington's 225th birthday, the local newspaper held an essay contest, asking children, "What do these important, famous words of Captain Lawrence mean to you today?"

"Making good choices," wrote one winner, "means that I cannot give up on what I believe. I have to decide what I stand for and keep working every day when problems come my way. Like Captain James Lawrence said, 'Don't give up the ship.' I cannot give up my ship which are [*sic*] the things that I believe in and stand for."

As a historian, Jeff Macechak advocates for a full understanding of the motto that was taken by Oliver Hazard Perry to the Great Lakes front of the War of 1812, eventually to become the motto of the world's most powerful navy. Whatever the actual words were, he says, it's important to remember that they were followed by another short sentence. The full utterance, in his understanding, was, "Don't give up the ship. Burn her!" If the fight was to be lost, the USS *Chesapeake* should be destroyed by its crew before it could be captured. Fortunately for the fullness of time, his last command was not followed.

Captain James Lawrence/Jeffrey Macechak listens to the music of the drum and fife band Don't Give Up the Ship in front of Lawrence House in Burlington, New Jersey. *Burlington County Historical Society.*

And, reminds the historian whose discipline must overcome sentimentality, this was not the real last exclamation of James Lawrence. He lingered for three days after the battle, and his final words, according to Jeff Macechak, could have been something like, "It's getting dark. Give me a glass of water," as he sailed north toward his first funeral in Halifax. "I think," said Jeff Macechak, "if he had lived longer, he would have been a more important person."

When the *New York Times* published its article about the cemetery in Halifax that was saved by a rediscovered history, the story filtered down to newspapers around the country and eventually fell under the eyes of Henry Posey, a fire chief in Memphis, Tennessee. It was June 2000. His first reaction was one of gratitude to the citizens of Halifax, who had saved a sacred place for fallen Americans, a place that no one in the United States had really known much about. But as he thought about it further, the implications of what had happened in Halifax became more profound. "Here were some people from Canada," he said, "trying to save something that we had forgotten: 188 prisoners of war! Here they were forgotten, no markers on their graves, and they were trying to save it."

In 2000, Henry Posey was also a senior master sergeant with the 164th civil engineering squadron of the Tennessee Air National Guard, and it happened that the squadron was about to leave for a joint exercise with Canadian forces near Halifax. Not a man accustomed to mulling things over, he knew that the cemetery had to be visited by his group, and he thought that doing so might

The War of 1812 brought naval conflict between England and the United States from the Atlantic into the Great Lakes, especially Lake Erie. It fell to young Oliver Hazard Perry to lead forces in Lake Erie that assembled battleships from regional timber and sailed them into confrontation with the enemy. Perry's ship was the USS *Lawrence*, named after his late friend James Lawrence. The ship's banner read, "Don't Give Up the Ship," and was hoisted as the two forces headed into battle on September 10, 1813. The *Lawrence* was severely damaged by the HMS *Detroit*, but Perry and the ship's banner made their way to the USS *Niagara*, which then brought about the surrender of the *Detroit*. The event was a turning point in the War of 1812. It would lead to the taking of Fort Detroit from the British, and the beginning of unfettered commercial development of northern Ohio. *The Mariners' Museum, Newport News, Virginia.*

help the city in its own deliberations about what should be done with it. He began to search out those in Halifax mentioned in the newspaper article, and found Guy MacLean at home late one evening. He said that he had read about the cemetery in his local newspaper, and asked if it would be possible for his group to hold a small memorial service when they arrived in Nova Scotia.

"It's often impressed me," said Guy MacLean, "how conscious Americans are of foreign burials of military…just generally a feeling that they mustn't be left alone, nobody left behind." Therein lay a small difference between the historic sensibilities of the United States and Canada, two neighbors very much similar, but in other ways very much different. In this case, Canada did not always memorialize its past in the more emotional tones of Americans. Some studies of Canadian history depict a low-key sense of nationalism, derived from the country's relative youth as a sovereign nation, and the extent of the wilderness that separates its provinces.

Another of those in Halifax who had worked to preserve the lost cemetery was Graham Read, a member of the city council who was instrumental in the decision to purchase the land from its prospective developers. Traveling in France one day, he had been surprised by his own reaction to a memorial to an event that had occurred during World War I.

Vimy Ridge in Pas-de-Calais, France, was a German stronghold in the opening years of the war, commanding a strategic view of the battlefields. In 1915, the French had suffered 15,000 casualties

Canadian soldiers after victory at Vimy Ridge, France, in 1915. *Library and Archives Canada/ Department of National Defence fonds/PA-001332.*

in trying to gain control of it, and were not successful. Two years later, Allied commanders gave the job to relatively untested Canadian forces. The Canadians looked at the challenge in a new way. They used balloons and microphones to learn the locations of most of the German guns. They dug tunnels that would allow the placement of mines at the German front lines. They created a physical replica of the battle space, and made sure that every individual soldier knew it well. After a week of shelling to soften up the enemy, 27,000 Canadians opened the battle on the morning of April 9. Three days later they took the ridge, suffering more than 10,000 casualties, including 3,598 deaths.

In a sense, the Battle of Vimy Ridge was similar in its effect to the *Chesapeake/Leopard* affair of 1807. Coming fifty years after the founding of a sovereign Canada, it was celebrated across the vast nation as a national achievement. Some at the time referred to it as the event that gave true birth to the nation. "It was our coming-of-age," said Guy MacLean.

One morning Graham Read was asleep on an overnight bus from Spain to England. It was an intercity bus with a close schedule, not a tour bus. But the Halifax city councilman awoke around 7:00 a.m. to hear the driver talking over the PA system. "We have a Canadian onboard, and we're approaching the Vimy memorial." He drove the bus right up to the end of the road in front of the structure and stopped in front of two monumental pylons, representing Canada and France, rising from a vast, stone platform. Among other things, the platform held the engraved names of more than eleven thousand Canadians with no known graves, killed in France.

"It was a really moving moment in my life," said Graham Read. "All of a sudden, tears were rolling down my face. Here this foreign country thinks so much of us, they could let us put this big thing here." He would understand the events that were about to unfold when Henry Posey asked if he and others could plan a memorial at Deadman's Island.

Guy MacLean called Mayor Fitzgerald the next morning, and the city was immediately put at the full service of the American guardsmen. "At the time," said Henry Posey, "I didn't really know what I wanted to do, except have some kind of a memorial service. So I got up there, and things kept growing." There was no easy land access to the cemetery, so Henry Posey was led through the bramble for his first look at the small place he had read about. "The feeling was overwhelming. These were American soldiers in a foreign country. It was a chance for us to show our respect. We don't want to leave them somewhere, and think that some harm or disrespect was being shown to them."

He determined that his group would be the first Americans to give the soldiers and sailors proper recognition for their sacrifice in a mostly forgotten war, and a memorial service was planned for week's end. "More than half of us are black," the master sergeant recalled, "and once they found out that there were buried

Left to right: Councilman Graham Read, Senior Master Sergeant Henry Posey and Guy MacLean. *Jack Hartnett.*

former slaves they bought into it. To a man, everyone wanted to participate."

"We started sitting down with each other, trying to figure it out. We were a civil engineering bunch, with all of the trades, bricklayers, electricians, the whole nine yards." They gained access to the cemetery through the brambles that surrounded it and prepared it for ceremony. They pushed 188 crisscrossed American and POW flag formations into the dirt at scattered intervals. An American flag that had flown over the White House was sent from Washington, and a Halifax flag was donated by the city. Representatives of a British regiment that had been stationed at The Citadel asked if they could participate.

A program for the ceremony was printed, its cover holding the Schetky painting of the USS *Chesapeake* and HMS *Shannon* coming into Halifax Harbour (as seen on the cover of this book).

The ceremony took place on the gray, cool morning of Friday, June 23, 2000. In attendance with the Americans and the British were representatives of Canada's navy and a Canadian color guard that marched toward the center of the island against the backdrop of the waters and floating yachts of the Arm. Unseen bagpipes of the Armed Forces of Canada played from within the heavy forest that had grown out of the hillside of anonymous graves. Then "Taps" was played by a member of the Salvation Army, and the bagpipes echoed again from the forest in the playing of "Amazing Grace." Tears fell on the cheeks of many as a chaplain led a prayer.

An estimated two hundred people were in attendance, including representatives of national and international media. The City

A color guard marches past Target Hill on Deadman's Island in ceremonies on June 23, 2000. The hill contains as many as four hundred anonymous burials, dating back to the turn of the nineteenth century. *Jack Hartnett.*

of Halifax spent $100,000 to create a path to the cemetery that could be used by its equipment. The event was broadcast across Canada, and Peter Jennings, a native Canadian, reported from the site for his *ABC Evening News* program in the United States. In a press conference afterward, Henry Posey summed up the intent behind what his squadron had accomplished in concert with the spontaneous participation of three nations that shared so much history. It was about the names that had been so dutifully recorded and preserved by the British Admiralty. "It starts to mean so much to you. You realize that they had families, they had homes, they had wants and needs that were never fulfilled. When you think that they have been here for 188 years and nothing has been done, it hurts in the heart."

"To stand there with them and see," said Guy MacLean, "how moved they were by this little ceremony they had put together—they did the whole thing. It was really far superior to any other official stuff that's happened since with dignitaries, cabinet ministers, ambassadors, that sort of thing."

There would be more to come for Deadman's Island. The squadron from the Tennessee Air National Guard had done the work that would further secure the cemetery's future. Years later, Graham Read, who would continue to take it down that path, looked back from the perspective of his own experience at Vimy Ridge. "I'm wondering if Posey and his group had the same experience here; and would they have the same experience walking on the planks of the *Chesapeake* itself, as a flour mill in England."

Media coverage focuses on the members of the 164th civil engineering squadron of the Tennessee Air National Guard, lined up in a cemetery they had helped return to life in Halifax, Nova Scotia. *Jack Hartnett.*

The moral imperative for the memorial service in Halifax had been right and true. There was nothing ambiguous about it. But the answer to the question of how Henry Posey and others might respond to the timbers of the USS *Chesapeake* in Wickham was more complicated. Curious Americans had shown up at the mill from time to time over its years. They had spurred young Eric Walker of Gosport into his lifelong study of the mill. Bruce Tappenden, the mill's historian and last private owner, told the tale that one day an anonymous American asked to be shown around the mill and was given a slice of its wood. Then a U.S. naval staff car showed up at the mill the following day to invite the miller and his wife to a luncheon onboard an American aircraft carrier in Portsmouth Harbour. The story is no doubt true, but its specifics are elusive.

After the County of Hampshire purchased the mill in 1998, the effort was begun to determine what should be done with it. John Wain, of the Britannia Naval Research Association, looks back on those several years as another complexity in the long history of Britain and the United States.

It was thought that the U.S. Navy would want to have a voice in the deliberation, and the navy was brought into it through the U.S. Embassy in London. John Wain said,

The American side used very careful protocol. I think they were embarrassed by it. Because I don't really think the U.S. Navy

The Meon River arrives at the Chesapeake Mill on its journey from the north. *The Chesapeake Mill.*

Another ship named USS *Chesapeake* served briefly in 1919, though her name was not given to her by the navy. The civilian freighter *Chesapeake* was built in 1900 by Harlan and Hollingsworth of Wilmington, Delaware. She was commissioned and refitted by the navy in March 1919 and sailed to France and Scotland, where she performed freight, salvage and minesweeping duties post–World War I. She was decommissioned in October of that year, and sold to British interests for salvage.

The second HMS *Chesapeake* was a screw-propelled, wooden frigate launched in 1855 at Chatham Dockyard. She saw action in the Second Opium War against the Quing Dynasty of China, was flagship of the British China Squadron in 1861 and was broken up in 1867.

wanted any part of celebrating the Chesapeake. *It's a difficult concept for some people to catch on to, but the* Chesapeake *is bad medicine for the U.S. Navy. So much so that they embargoed ever using that name for a ship again, and that does resound down the decades. I think it's difficult for the Brits to understand that.*

I find with some Americans that you tell them the story, but they don't really want to make a big thing about it. But from our point of view, it's a hands across the sea thing. And it's not a celebration; it's a recognition of absolute stupidity, especially as it stems from the Chesapeake/Leopard *affair.*

Wain called the 1807 event a brazen attack on what was known to be a defenseless ship. "A defenseless ship," he repeated, "and we just went ahead and did it!"

On the civilian side, however, it was a group of naval historians from all three nations that had been touched by the *Chesapeake* that took up the cause. They were led by Dr. Robert Prescott of the University of St. Andrews, Scotland, a preeminent authority on maritime history and the ships on which it was borne.

In the matter of the Chesapeake Mill, Robert Prescott was chief advocate of its importance to the past and future of naval archaeology. "This mill contains one of the best preserved 18th-century warships in the world," he was quoted as saying in the *Ottawa Citizen* on October 13, 2003. "The building has protected these timbers in extraordinary condition. When you walk through, you still feel like you're on a ship. And when the wind's blowing, well…"

The article, one of a very few pieces of reporting on the plight of the mill in North America, went on to recount the battle of the *Chesapeake* and *Shannon* from a Canadian perspective. "The seizing of the *Chesapeake*," it reported, "was a tremendous blow to U.S. morale and an inspiration to Canadian and British troops, who in 1814 finally repulsed the attempted American invasion of the country."

In 2003, the Chesapeake Mill, and the ship within, came to the fork in the road to its future. On one path lay a different version of the failed Environmental and Heritage Center of the 1990s in the form of a museum devoted to the common naval heritage of three nations, and the history of a British water mill. On the other path lay the practical view of a county council that owned an old building that, in its view, needed to be supported by commercial enterprise.

"I'm pretty sure we have the most museums of any county in the country," said Gary Carroll of the County of Hampshire's Department of Estates Planning. "They are very expensive to

Chesapeake timbers in the mill before the refurbishment of 2003. It is likely that the facing vertical cuts in each of the two beams were part of the ship's interlocking (dado and rebate) construction. *Jeffrey Macechak.*

After refurbishment, many of the timbers are whitewashed, but some researchers see the battle damage of pockmarks and bloodstains in the wood. The New York Times magazine supplement of May 22, 1898, reported that "upon the floors, the walls, and the rafters overhead are seen huge, dark patches, as though at some time, blood had stagnated there; and there are small holes in the timbers which, when probed with a penknife, give up round balls of lead which fall to the floor with a thud, or strike softly upon the flour sacks beneath." *Eric Walker.*

run. Visitor numbers are not as great as they used to be, and our most popular museums find it difficult to make ends meet." It was commercial activity, he pointed out, that was increasingly becoming the financial underpinning of historic buildings worldwide. "Officers and Members of the County Council believed the best way to keep the property going was to find a new commercial use that would be sensitive to the building and look after it, keep it going for many years to come." Their stated goal was to attain a quality refurbishment and preservation of the mill's historic features and machinery, accompanied by an appropriate level of public access to the building.

In April 2003, the council, saying that it could not afford the approximate £1 million necessary to repair and preserve the mill, announced that it was up for sale as a leasehold, the county retaining ownership. "The County Council fully recognizes," said council leader Ken Thornber, "the importance of the property, not only locally, but nationally and internationally, particularly in the USA." With the announcement of the sale, the county

A recycled stairway from the USS *Chesapeake?* It was the practice, said Eric Walker, to replace worn stairways in wooden ships by reversing them. A dendochronological test of the wood could confirm its age. *Jeffrey Macechak, right; Eric Walker, opposite.*

produced a planning brief that it felt would safeguard the building's architectural and historic features while ensuring public access to at least a portion of it. The wish was to find a commercial use for the building that would complement its historic value. "Such use will need to be economically viable in its own right and able to safeguard the Mill in the long term."

Those who wanted the mill preserved as a historical building were immediately returned to the visions of the building as a restaurant (there had been discussion about a pizzeria) or office building that had first arisen in the 1990s. "I'm horrified by this," said the chairman of the Hampshire Mills Group, John Silman. "The mill is a desperately, historically-important mill. When the Council first bought it, it was going to be an interpretation centre for the Meon Valley." It appeared that those kinds of plans were

Exceeding Chivalry?

The *New York Times* magazine supplement of May 22, 1898, published an article about the *Chesapeake* quoting an unnamed "English writer who ardently desires a permanent bond of union between the two great divisions of the Anglo-Saxon family." The reporting, containing factual errors in other regards, suggested that Lawrence had been done in by compassion.

"Lawrence displayed great skill and tactics while closing at 5:50 P.M. He luffed up and backed his mainyard when within fifty feet of the Shannon's weather-quarter; he might have wore down across the stern of Broke's frigate and raked her from stern to stem. But he refrained. That was magnificent—it was chivalrous to the highest degree – so high as to be beyond the realm of common sense. "And so it seems that Englishmen are right, after all, in attributing to Lawrence a touch of the spirit of old-time knight errantry."

going to be dashed again, and that the council, which had bought the mill in 1998 to preserve it from commercial forces, was now prepared to sell it to those same forces in 2003.

The uproar arose from an alliance of historians, academics and citizens of Wickham who accused the council of stripping the assets of a historic building that was probably unique in the world. One angry member of the group, reported the *Independent*, claimed that the council had betrayed the villagers and historians who valued the mill's history, and had deliberately sunk the effort to save the building for the nation's history.

"It's a sop…a great shame," said one of its supporters, reflecting a fear that once a new leasehold was granted, it could be renegotiated to a further deterioration of the mill's historic features. In the same article, villager Mark Phillimore was quoted in a provocative speculation that would endure long after the matter was settled. "More of the original timbers of the *Chesapeake* are in the mill than exist from any other historic ship. Thirty per cent of the original timbers of the *Chesapeake* are in that building—only 5 per cent of HMS *Victory* is original. The whole selling process is unnecessarily speedy."

The battle was then joined by the reappearance, once again, of the USS *Chesapeake*. In the spirit of saving the ship within the mill, a meeting was called at the National Maritime Museum in Greenwich. Among those in attendance were Robert Prescott and representatives of the Maritime Museum and the Royal Naval Museum of the United Kingdom; the North American Society for Oceanic History, the U.S. Naval Institute, the National Maritime Historical Society and the National Maritime Alliance of the United States; and the Canadian Nautical Research Society. Official United States interests were represented through the defense attaché of the London embassy in the person of Adriane de Savorgnani, formerly the commander of U.S. naval medical clinics in the United Kingdom, and an advocate for the *Chesapeake*. It was her belief that in the matter of the battle with the *Shannon*, James Lawrence had not "acquitted himself very well. We shouldn't really have lost that good ship. But we did." She had been involved in bringing Canadian interests to the table, "to bring more or less a tri-partite front to an effort to try to preserve the mill for posterity, for its history and all the rest." There was no representation from the U.S. Navy.

It was John Silman's recollection that Robert Prescott brought excitement to the meeting with a stunning announcement. "Prescott really did lay it on the line. He said 'Look, we've discovered since the last discussion that two American frigates, the USS *Constellation* and the USS *Constitution* are rebuilds, and they've got no more than 5% of the original timbers in them. We reckon we've got 35% of the original timbers in Chesapeake Mill.'" Those figures, and those of Mark Phillimore of Wickham, remained to be confirmed.

The expression of the Chesapeake Action Group (CAG) was to impress upon the County of Hampshire the wish that the mill be turned into a heritage-based organization. "Our proposal is to conserve and interpret this extraordinary monument in a museum and heritage center," said Robert Prescott. "It's an astonishing building of international significance as the War of 1812 between England and America is often forgotten." It was noted that the bicentennial of the war would be coming along in several years, and that a place for its interpretation would be valuable to that important anniversary. The interpretation of the mill itself, Robert Prescott commented, would be of the "extraordinary transformation of the sanguinary man-o'-war into the life-preserving producer of grain…a metaphorical beating of swords into plough-shares."

The proposal, and a business plan that would support it, was hand delivered to the Hampshire County Council in July 2003. The council agreed to delay its decision on the sale of the leasehold for two months to allow the preservationists to fulfill the underpinnings of their plan. But soon thereafter the optimism shared by John Silman and others after the meeting in Greenwich was dashed. There was no money to be raised from English sources.

"There's so much history around here competing for money," said Barrie Marson of the Wickham History Society. "I think the chance of getting lottery funding [a traditional supporter of historic preservation] or any other funding for that matter would have been less than 50/50. People see more important places, old churches, naval installations. There's all this dockyards stuff of course which needs preservation." As in past years, furtive appeals were made to American sensibilities. "Letters were written to American institutions which all produced a lot of interest. Everyone wished them well, but didn't provide any support." The U.S. Navy, recalled Barrie Marson, reflected an interest in the project, but did not follow through with actual support.

"The basic answer to the question 'what happened?'" said John Silman, "is really that nothing happened." And on October 16, the county council announced a decision that would, on its face, reach well into the twenty-second century:

Historic Plastervation?

According to *A Calendar of Papers of Josiah Fox* in the collection of Ernest J. Wesson, Mansfield, Ohio, 1935, Josiah Fox preserved copies of the drafts of every ship built by him. They fell into the possession of his grandchildren, however, and the plans for the *Constitution* ended up as a cover for a kitchen ironing board. A plasterer found a box of plans of the others in the attic and, thinking they were wallpaper remnants, set them afire to dry a just plastered room.

COUNTY COUNCIL SAVES CHESAPEAKE MILL

Hampshire County Council has announced its plans to save Chesapeake Mill, Wickham after it considered in detail a scheme submitted by a heritage group Chesapeake Action Group (CAG) along with the preferred commercial bid which was selected in July. Unusually the County Council agreed to provide an additional two months for the heritage bid to be submitted.

The County Council acquired the Mill in 1998 to protect the historic integrity of the building which for nearly 200 years has been used as a commercial flour mill. The County Council commenced marketing of the Mill in March 2003 but the heritage group did not make clear their intention to bid until July.

Since this time a group of people with local, national and international connections has assembled proposals for the Mill based around the creation of an interpretive centre. The preferred commercial bid was for the use of the building for the restoration and retailing of antiques and would involve taking a lease from the County Council who would retain the freehold of the Mill.

The prospective leaseholders Taylor Haimes Ltd. indicated their willingness to work with local interest groups to provide a museum area within the Mill and to make the building available for historical research as well as organised visits.

In arriving at the decision to accept the Taylor Haimes Ltd. bid, the Leader of the County Council, Councillor Ken Thornber, considered that the commercial use of the building offered a sustainable long-term use of the building whilst also providing access for people wanting to visit the Mill and to carry out historical research. The County Council has extensive experience of operating museums and was not convinced that the CAG proposals offered a viable solution for the long-term protection of the Mill.

The matter was settled. The timbers—which had been brought together in Virginia's Gosport Shipyard in 1799, played a catalytic role in the development of a new nation, fought pirates in the Mediterranean and the British on the Atlantic, twice touched the heart of Halifax and fed the people and animals of a British county—would become an antique mall.

"I am not surprised, but it is very disappointing," said Reverend Geoffrey Morrell of the Chesapeake Action Group, calling the decision a victory of commerce over community. That sentiment wasn't universal, however. "I think most people appreciated the fact

The Chesapeake Mill receives a new roof under the terms of a new leasehold on life. *The Chesapeake Mill.*

that the county had done it," said Barrie Marson. "We wrote to the county asking for assurance that it wouldn't be sold simply to a speculator who would take money out of it. And the county assured us that they would have our interests at heart, and only sell it with constraints on its future use. Which is what they've done."

"To some extent it turned out better than we anticipated," said Tony Yarrow of the Hampshire Mills Group, "and to some extent worse. We were disappointed that it wasn't to become an interpretation center." But they formed an agreement with the new owner that would allow them to look after and preserve the mill equipment still in the building. Yarrow said, "Our hope is that somebody will take on the job that we're doing, or I fear for the future of the mill."

Some years after the decision, Gary Carroll of the County of Hampshire's Department of Estates Planning remembered that the desire of the county was to open the mill to public access, which it had not actually allowed since 1820, and to see it used in keeping with its historic nature in a way that would not require the construction of an interior redesign. The antique and gift mall, in his view, met those goals perfectly.

He pointed out a simple but powerful fact of the matter. The mill had survived as a commercial enterprise for more than 150 years, "and we wanted the mill to go back into a commercial use, as it's always been." Indeed, when the building was acquired by Taylor Haimes, the first order of business was to invest over £100,000 in a new roof that would continue to protect the timbers within.

Left to right: Tony Yoward, John Silman and Nigel Smith (in the floor) of the Hampshire Mills Group fix the jammed main drive shaft of Chesapeake Mill as it rises from the turbine and through the ground floor. *Hampshire Mills Group.*

The January 2004 editorial in England's *Telegraph* that asked to be forgiven by dendrophiles for suggesting that a plank was just a plank was timely and provocative. "A commercial role might be just as much of an asset to the community as a didactic one," it went on to say. "Whatever happens, the listing regulations should prevent the building from substantial alteration. It is not as if the timbers reward repeated scrutiny; surely it's enough to know that they're there, and they're safe. The teens of Wickham would probably prefer an amusement arcade."

The disposition of the remnants of the USS *Chesapeake*, and the memorializing of a handful of her sailors among other casualties of war, may have much to tell us about the ways we will honor history in a new century. The *Chesapeake* timbers have been in a safe place for almost two hundred years only because they were the prize of a recycling nation, and came into the possession of an enterprising miller of grain. It may be that the necessity of recycling carried a wisdom for the ages.

Just at the time that the Chesapeake Mill came to the fork in the road to its future, many of those who work in the field of historic interpretation and preservation were finding themselves in need of new road maps. "Chesapeake Mill as a museum," said Gary Carroll of the English county in which the Chesapeake had come to rest, "would have been incredibly expensive to refurbish using county council money, added to which it's a very expensive building to keep running."

The same reality was coming to light in the community from which the *Chesapeake* had been launched in 1799. The Mariners' Museum in Newport News, Virginia, is one of the world's great resources for the interpretation and study of maritime history, but, like the museums of the County of Hampshire, it was beginning to find that, in a time of dramatic development of new kinds of entertainment and educational products, fewer visitors were coming through its doors. Artifacts and exhibitions seemed to be losing their drawing power, and the reason for that might be a different version of the question that is asked about the timbers in Chesapeake Mill: what are they, actually?

William Cogar, a maritime historian, author and expert on the War of 1812, became the Mariners' Museum's executive vice-president and chief operating officer in 2008. Though he had not seen the *Chesapeake* timbers, and had not been given the opportunity to experience what other historians have called the sense of walking into the soul of a ship in Chesapeake Mill, he thought of them in the same way that motivated John Prior to use their shape and size to build his new water mill. "I perceive that somebody very wisely took advantage of superb timber, and that's great. Somebody saw this golden opportunity, and took it."

William Cogar also perceived that at the beginning of a new era of digital interaction and virtual worlds, the artifacts of the past might need to be thought of in new ways. "I have to be careful about

Figurehead restorer Eric Walker's recreation of the billet head of the USS *Chesapeake*. A billet head was often used in place of a figurehead at the prow of a ship. The billet head of the USS *Chesapeake* was nearly seven feet tall, of black painted wood with gold painted trim and is owned by an American collector. *Eric Walker.*

going too far in the preservation of historical objects, and not lose sight of what is functional. As a museum, we need to question their sustainability when resources dry up. We cannot and should not do everything to save them. It requires us to make tough decisions."

As an example, he cited the common situation in which naval veterans of World War II learn that a particular kind of ship in their experience is in danger of breaking, and fight to have it preserved as the holder of their stories and memories, leaving future generations to support something with which they have no personal connection. "We have to be more selective, and we're caught between a rock and a hard place. We can't invest in something without the sustainability to back it up."

The future of the Mariners' Museum, with its tremendous resources of knowledge, records and information, and similar museums is being pushed into virtual worlds that may predominate over artifacts in glass cases—even the most creative of interactive exhibits within museum walls. Virtual preservation and documentation may yield more knowledge over time than physical objects that must be stored and protected. "We're looking at a paradigm shift to be sustainable as an institution. We have to change, use everything now available to enhance research and access to what we have, world wide. We can do that now," Cogar said. It may be that the next recycling of some historic objects will be into their virtual duplicates.

That view is balanced on the other side of Hampton Roads harbor, as Corey Thornton of the Norfolk Naval Shipyard Museum answered the question of the timbers that he, too, is yet to see. He said,

> *They are, physical evidence of an historical series of situations, a part of the* Chesapeake *that has managed to stick around. There's an essence there that requires thinking about where has this been? What was it like for the people aboard? All kinds of questions come to mind. It's just this physical thing and you know it has a story.*
>
> *It's hard to put into words, but I'm thinking that it does have a soul. I fully agree with that. It has an essence to it that tells its own story, in addition to the historical facts.*

Though given life in the shipyard that his museum commemorates, Corey Thornton felt that Wickham probably held the greater claim on the *Chesapeake*. "She was born here, and in a perfect world she would return here. But she seems to be more revered over there, and I say Amen to that. But if they called us up and said we could have the timbers back, we'd try to get them. We have a moral responsibility to keep her story alive by keeping her remaining artifacts alive."

The stories that would be told by the *Chesapeake* timbers would be those of the people who sailed with her and fought her battles. At the same time that objects may be giving up their sustainability, the memory of people associated with them seems to become more important. That had been the firm motivation of Henry Posey and his group from Tennessee when the people of Halifax cleared the way for a memorial service on Deadman's Island in 2000. Those two hundred people of three nations with their bagpipes and kilts, flags and prayers led to yet another, more traditional, form of remembrance.

Guy MacLean said,

> *Henry Posey's phone call set a number of things in motion. Otherwise we'd probably still have a little green hummock over there with a small sign on it saying, "What you're looking at is the site of some burials from the War of 1812." The fact that that night Jennings was on* ABC News *reporting on the thing, it was on the* CBC *and* CTV Evening News *that night from the little island, embarrassed the city government and the staff people who said, "My God. This is an important little thing that's developed here."*
>
> *Having purchased the unkempt island, the city knew that it had to now make public access possible, and it needed to put up a marker of some sort.*

The matter came to the attention of the U.S. Veteran's Administration in Washington, D.C. Normal policy held that when buried veterans were found in foreign lands they were to be disinterred and reburied at Arlington Cemetery, but the commingling of graves without markers on Deadman's Island made that impossible, so plans were put in place in 2003 to create a memorial marker similar to one that would have been placed at Arlington. A fully landscaped path down the hill and through the woods was built by the city, with access from a residential street. Benches were installed overlooking the waters of the Northwest Arm.

Henry Posey had started the ball rolling, but it was really the people of Halifax who picked up from the memorial service in 2000. Ever the promoter of green space, Guy MacLean began

The Armdale Yacht Club, formerly the warder's house, watches Deadman's Island from Melville Island in the Northwest Arm. *Frances J. Beck.*

referring to the cemetery as an "international historic site," though there is no legal definition and standing for such places in Canada. "It was, as far as we were concerned," said Guy MacLean with a conspiratorial laugh. And though it was never approved as an official national historic site in Canada, it came to be considered a place of international heritage by the city of Halifax. In 2004, planning was begun to preserve the cemetery in a final way. The U.S. Consulate became involved, and Canada's Maritime Forces Atlantic joined with American military forces in the province at the center of an effort reported to be the undertaking of hundreds of people in two countries.

On May 29, 2005, *Halifax Daily News* reporter Ruth Davenport, referring to a *Chesapeake* sailor, offered a preview of what would happen the following day.

> *No one noticed when John Johnson died for his country. There was no pomp or ceremony for the 22-year-old seaman from New York. No headstone, no 21-gun salute, no burial at sea for the young American who died on June 12, 1813…The USS Constitution still floats in Boston Harbour, as imposing today as when she battled the daunting British navy. But Johnson and 187 other American prisoners of war lie forgotten on the pine covered knoll in Halifax's Northwest Arm, their bones tangled ignominiously in the marshy ground.…No one noticed when Johnson died for his country, but with the burden of guilt on their minds, his modern countrymen are making sure no one forgets.*

May 30 was the American Memorial Day. "The people of Halifax," said U.S. naval commander Brad Renner, "are going to

A monument to the forgotten of Deadman's Island, placed by the U.S. Veteran's Administration in 2005. *Frances J. Beck.*

enable us to do something that, for the last 200 years, we haven't been able to do. And that is to remember and mourn these guys and to keep alive the spirit of service to your country, no matter how great the cost."

The second ceremony at Deadman's Island brought together officials of both countries. British reenactors of the Seventy-eighth Highland Regiment were joined by members of the Kings Orange Rangers, whose group had protected Nova Scotia against American privateers in the Revolutionary War; a color guard from the *Chesapeake*'s sister ship USS *Constitution*; and sailors of the HMCS *Charlottetown*, which had distinguished herself in World War II. Bagpipes and "Taps" were played. The American flag was folded and given to Halifax Mayor John Kelley. "Our commitment," he said, "to you, the people of the U.S. of America in this, the Year of the Veteran, is as we honour our own veterans, we will also honour yours."

"It's hard for me to imagine this happening in any other country," said the U.S. Embassy's charge d'affairs, John Dickson. "Canada and the U.S. have come a huge distance since 1812, and we serve as an example to the world."

The ultimate recognition of the sacred place came as the U.S. Veteran's Administration placed its claim on the once-forgotten soldiers and sailors of Deadman's Island with a six- by eight-foot bronze plaque engraved with the names of 188 fallen American prisoners of war. Mounted on a granite base, it rises just slightly from the earth to the sky, and is visited by many of the few Americans who know about it. Whenever a U.S. naval ship comes into Halifax, a group of its sailors travel up the hill from the harbour, past the citadel on the city's highest spot and down Quinpool Road to attend to the grounds of a once-forgotten burial place.

If the year 2005 brought a good resolution to the future of those lain to rest on Deadman's Island, it was the year that the Chesapeake Mill in Wickham, the County of Hampshire, was fully returned to life. In November 2004 the *Hampshire Chronicle* had headlined a story about the successful grand opening of the new antique, jewelry and gift mall: "Chesapeake Mill 'sets sale' again!" The refurbishment

The Chesapeake Mill.

of the mill by Taylor Haimes included restoration of an ancient turbine that, the following February, was able once again to tap into the force of the Meon River and drive a generator that brought electricity and light to the upper floors.

A few years later, Gary Carroll of the County of Hampshire's Department of Estates Planning viewed the venture as a success. "It works very well as a commercial building. A lot of people are going there not just because they know the Chesapeake story, but because Wickham is a very attractive village. People come to enjoy it, and when they get to the mill they learn about its history. If it had just been a museum, there would probably be far less numbers coming through it."

The issue seemed to be moot with naval historians. The effort to create a museum had been tried, but failed, and, after initial unhappiness, there seemed to be some satisfaction that the ship within the building, with vigilance, would be preserved—if not for the full length of a 125-year lease, at least until the next challenge came along, if ever. The historian Robert Prescott had moved on from Wickham, and distinguished himself in 2004 with the discovery in an Essex marsh of the skeleton of the HMS *Beagle*, the ship that had taken Charles Darwin into his exploration of a theory of evolution in the 1830s.

In September 2007, Wickham was chosen as winner of the County of Hampshire's annual "Hampshire Village of the Year" competition, and would go on to compete for the title of Britain's "Village of the Year." The old watermill constructed of a nineteenth-century American warship was listed near the top of Wickham's many accomplishments. It probably augurs well for at least another century in the life of the USS *Chesapeake*. With smoke alarms screwed into her timbers, and built rugged for battles at sea, she sits peacefully solid beside a small but roaring river—the "unlucky ship," but perhaps the luckiest of them all. And one that will always have a good story to tell.

AFTERWORD

One of the unrealized goals of the writing of this book has been to answer a question that may not ultimately be very important: now in the twenty-first century, is there more of the original USS *Chesapeake* in Wickham, England, than there is original USS *Constitution* in Boston Harbor? And if there were, what would that mean? How one considers those questions might depend on how one responds to the provocative assertion by the *Daily Telegraph* of England, with which the story began, "Mystically communing with objects which have been in interesting places will only get you so far."

Then there is the question that arises out of the situations in which museums and other historical sites find themselves these days: do we devote precious resources to the preservation and interpretation of actual relics, or do we recycle them into virtual relics that can be more universally accessed and examined?

Historic ships, though, are a bit different from museums. They are preserved environments, rather than static exhibitions. Thus they can create the sense, reported by maritime historians, and felt by this author, of walking into "the soul of a ship" while poking around in an old English water mill.

From the standpoint of preservation, the most striking difference between the USS *Constitution* and whatever of the USS *Chesapeake* that resides in the old water mill is that the *Constitution* is a product of a continuous restoration using new materials while the remains of the *Chesapeake* are just as they were in 1820, and, given the protection of walls and a roof, never restored.

Some may think it would be interesting, even exciting, to know which of the two constructions has more original material, while others may think it to be a question with no purpose. Whichever, it could be a fascinating investigation for those who are interested in such things. But there is currently no known prospect of the investigation ever happening.

Here is what is both known and speculated. When the matter of preserving the mill became most urgent to historians in 2003, the effort was led by Dr. Robert Prescott, who had made a presentation in September 2002 to the British Association's festival of science at the University of Leicester. "All the beams over your head," he said, "which hold up the floor above you are gun-deck and quarter-deck beams from the ship, and all the lintels that span the openings of doors and windows are from the ship."

Dr. Prescott is acknowledged in the United States and Britain as a preeminent naval historian, and his words are taken as gospel by many who have been involved in the story of the *Chesapeake*. His study of the mill was presumably thorough, informed and academically rigorous. John Silman of the Hampshire Mills Group recalls Dr. Prescott telling a meeting at the National Maritime Museum in Greenwich that 30 percent of the Chesapeake was in the mill (page 141), and that was repeated by an ally of Dr. Prescott's, described in newspaper accounts as a Wickham villager, as a talking point in the effort to preserve the mill as a museum (page 140).

Unfortunately, Dr. Prescott, who is presumed to have the best knowledge of what of the USS *Chesapeake* is in Chesapeake Mill, has not responded to questions about his research to this author, either directly or through intermediaries, and to others who have tried to talk with him in recent years. Some speculate that he will be writing a book on the subject at the time of the War of 1812 bicentennial, and if that is the case it will be a valuable addition to the story, indeed.

Not everyone agreed with the 30 percent figure at the time it first surfaced. Members of the British Naval Research Association said at the time, "Our research suggests that less than two per cent of the original *Chesapeake* timbers survive in the mill, identifiable by their construction marks and joint housings. There are only 14 identifiable deck beams used to support the mill's floors: the original ship had some 118 deck beams." They went on to say, however, "The BNRA strongly believes that the Chesapeake Mill should attract World Heritage Site status as Portsmouth's fourth historic vessel, given Wickham's proximity to the Historic Dockyard. We hope this research will encourage all groups to work together to secure the mill's preservation."

But subsequent visits to the mill's cut and uncut wood created an increasingly open-ended answer to the question. John Wain of the BNRA said in 2007,

It seemed on each of our visits, more timber would come into the equation as it was assessed and there were areas which

were difficult to access on adhoc visits as entry to the mill at this time was on a limited basis. It was a fair bet that the refashioned timber was also Chesapeake, *but, in the main, only archaeological methods of identification were going to supply answers here and this was the value of Robert Prescott's survey which we believe was exhaustive. But we still haven't seen sight of the findings, only hearsay reports of them.*

The proportion of material from Chesapeake *may not be the big issue, what is crucial is that the beams are identifiable and can be placed in the structure of the ship.*

And in all of the discussion of original content in recent years, there has always been a potential trap in the use of language. Perhaps what Robert Prescott actually said was that 30 percent of the mill was made of *Chesapeake* wood, rather than 30 percent of the *Chesapeake* was in the mill. Various percentages seem to have been presented in both ways, creating confusion over a figure that may ultimately be unknowable.

The USS *Constitution* is deemed the only one of the six frigates still with us. The question of the origins of the USS *Constellation* in Baltimore has been the subject of other books and debates. Official estimates of the *Constitution*'s original material range from 13 to 20 percent, but Patrick Otton, technical writer for the Naval Historical Center Detachment in Boston during the 1990s, said that percentages are meaningless in this kind of discussion.

"It is," he said, "constantly repeated about the *Constitution* that she's 13% original, but 13% of what? What's the calculation you've done to come up with the number 13?" The determination, he says, has to come through the independent study of units of the ship through weight, volume or specific original condition.

The Chesapeake Mill is as it was in 1820, a large portion of a U.S. Navy frigate turned into a water mill. But over the course of several rebuilds and restorations the *Constitution* has changed both in content and purpose. The structural needs of a heroic warship are much different than those of a national monument, and changes have followed that evolution in the ship's mission.

Patrick Otton said, "I could take the time and calculate volume or something like that and probably say what percentage of the total ship is original, but you're probably going to be disappointed. It's going to end up being a few tenths of a percent. The *Constitution* is 2000 tons, and we're not talking ten percent of that in that structure."

Keel
A large beam from bow to stern that serves as the spine of the ship, and from which the hull is built. Joshua Humphreys: "Of good sound white oak."

Stem
The upright member mounted on the forward end of the keel, to which longitudinal planks (strakes) are attached from stem to stern. Joshua Humphreys: "In two pieces, if to be had; the lower one of good white oak."

Futtocks
Pieces of timber bent and bolted together, and risen up to shape the body of the ship. Joshua Humphreys: "Of live oak, sided twelve inches in the midship and something smaller at the fore and after ends of the ship."

Patrick Otton's understanding of the *Constitution* is based on his own research, matched with available repair records for the ship.

> *In all likelihood, in looking at repairs to the* Constitution *as the Navy knew them at the time I was working, the keel and lower futtocks are probably still original. The keelson certainly has been added to several times, but a replacement of the lower futtocks and keel would have been recorded in the repair history of the ship, and those records don't exist. Replacing the gundeck, the lower deck, the spar deck, replacing the upper futtocks and all the spars and rigging—with confidence you can say that that stuff is not original. What is original in the* Constitution *in my estimate is the stern post, lower stem, the keel and the lower futtocks. Everything else has been replaced.*

Is there a point to the question of the original *Chesapeake* versus the original *Constitution*? Would it lead to a great American national awakening about one of its treasures now in England? "There may be a reasonable argument to be made about it," said Patrick Otton, "but it's not going to draw anyone's attention here. It's just hard enough to keep the Constitution supported and repaired."

The final word, for the time being, goes by default to Eric Walker, who discovered the mill as "a curious little boy" and spent a lifetime studying its innards while in the Royal Navy, and in an avocation as a ship and figurehead restorer. He has questioned the little things that might otherwise escape notice, like the possibly reversed stairway of the original ship (page 138), and considered the larger context of the *Chesapeake*'s breaking in 1819. He figured that if all of the *Chesapeake* timbers that are claimed to be in the buildings of lower Hampshire County were somehow gathered up, there would be more than enough to rebuild the HMS *Victory*. Most of them, he asserts, were in the houses and furniture destroyed in the air raids of World War II, some of them recycled into subsequent rebuilding.

His personal and unofficial inventory of the mill, however, is specific in what he thinks still remains, limited to the parts of the mill he has been able to survey as fully as he'd like.

Athwartship (width of ship) beams in the full structure
    14" x 11" x 33.5', 5 of yellow American pine
Mill bottom floor beams
    13" x 15" x 33.5', 30 of yellow American pine

Mill upstairs floor beams
    14" x 11" x 33.5', 5 of yellow American pine
    13" x 15" x 33.5', 2 of yellow American pine
Mill top floor beams
    14" x 11" x 33.5', 6 of yellow American pine, estimated
On top of support beams
    Floorboards in the mill may be a mix of original and machine-sawn wood of a later date
Elsewhere
    9" x 3" x 8' Lintels, 5 in number from gun deck

Other observations have produced other results. If the truth of the matter is important, it's still pending.

In the meantime, whatever of the *Chesapeake*'s timbers rest in the Chesapeake Mill, the Englishman Eric Walker suggests an inventory that all can agree upon: "As the American crews mortally shed their blood on the ship's timbers, the timbers indeed have a soul, and the ship lives in spirit."

Please visit www.theusschesapeake.com and www.theenduringjourney.com for links, sources and conversation related to material in this book. Join us in a continuing exploration into the world of the USS *Chesapeake*.

Visit us at
www.historypress.net